# Presidential Power in Latin American Politics

edited by
# Thomas V. DiBacco

The Praeger Special Studies program—utilizing the most modern and efficient book production techniques and a selective worldwide distribution network—makes available to the academic, government, and business communities significant, timely research in U.S. and international economic, social, and political development.

# Presidential Power in Latin American Politics

PRAEGER SPECIAL STUDIES IN INTERNATIONAL POLITICS AND GOVERNMENT

**Praeger Publishers**   New York   London

Library of Congress Cataloging in Publication Data

Main entry under title:

Presidential power in Latin American politics.

   (Praeger special studies in international politics
and government)
   Includes index.
   1. Executive power—Latin America—Addresses,
essays, lectures.  2.  Latin America—Presidents—
Addresses, essays, lectures.  I.  DiBacco, Thomas V.
JL961.P73   1977        351'.0032'098        77-4727
ISBN 0-03-021816-0

PRAEGER PUBLISHERS
200 Park Avenue, New York, N.Y. 10017, U.S.A.

Published in the United States of America in 1977
by Praeger Publishers, Inc.

789 038 987654321

Printed in the United States of America

Perhaps more than any other political office and institution, the presidency and the presidential system represent unique American contributions to the practice of government. The word "president" was first used in the United States to signify the presiding officers of the various conventions or congresses, and in Spanish America to refer to the presiding officer for the *audiencia,* or advisory council. Under the Articles of Confederation, ratified in 1781 as the first form of government for the newly-independent North American colonies, the president was the presiding officer of the congress; however, under Article II of the constitution written in Philadelphia in 1787, he became a constitutional executive, functioning as the head of state and of the government, independent of the congress.

The U. S. founding fathers were not always happy with the term "president" as it emerged after 1781, but it seemed preferable to "governor," the colonial and state counterpart to a national chief executive, about which there were memories of strife and confrontation. The substitution of the term "president" did not solve the problem of power that had contributed—through the offices of governor and king—to the coming of the revolution, for the president could be considered as either an executive officer in a republic or as an elected head of state having some of the functions of a constitutional monarch. The preference of some members of the first congress in 1789 for the title, "His Highness, the President of the United States, and Protector of the Rights of Same," is indicative of the tone of constitutional monarchs, as are also the conscious choices of the terms *consul* by Paraguay and *director* by Chile and Argentina in their postindependence years.

The free-flowing debates during the period of the American Revolution did not define precisely the boundaries of executive power. A dichotomy existed: on one side stood Thomas Paine and Benjamin Franklin arguing for a system in which a plural executive body would be subservient to the legislature (preferably unicameral); on the other side stood John Adams insisting on a separate executive with a fixed term of office and a strong veto power. Between these poles there was considerable variation of opinion regarding degrees of presidential power.

Nor was the question adequately settled by the Constitutional Convention in 1787. True, the president's powers would not be those of the British king, but they were nevertheless extensive: in contrast to the state governors, who would probably be selected by the legislature and ineligible for reelection, the president was not to be selected by Congress unless there were no majority in the electoral college. The president, moreover, was eligible for a second or subsequent term, could control his cabinet officers and even dismiss them, and did not serve at the pleasure of the legislature. In fact, he could be removed from office only "on impeachment for and conviction of treason, bribery, or other high crimes and misdemeanors." The absolute boundaries of the president's power were not defined in the Constitution: a clause allowing for the delegation of additional powers by Congress had been deleted at the Convention. However, the president's veto power, although not absolute, was greater than that of the vast majority of state governors; and one part thereof—the pocket veto—was unique in providing the president with a passive form of proscription of legislative matters.

In spite of its obvious ambiguities with respect to power, the U. S. presidency had a profound effect upon the Latin American nations—especially those of Spanish America emerging as independent states in the early nineteenth century. Not that the Latin American nations were similar to the United States in historical evolution toward reception of a presidency functioning in a republic. To be sure, the differences between the two areas were far greater than the similarities. Spanish and Portuguese America, for example, had been influenced by their own traditions, especially Spain's liberal constitution of 1812. Also, the independence movement in Latin America was distinct from the English example highlighted by its limited monarchy of 1689 and carried on by the legislature. Most importantly, the concept of federalism was interpreted differently in the two areas, with the U. S. version one of centralization (compensating for the state's rights emphasis of the Confederation period) and the Latin American version one of decentralization, as a reaction to the wide-ranging authority of the Spanish viceroys.

The populations of both Latin America and the United States were heterogeneous; but the Indians and mestizos were far more numerous in Spanish America, as were the enslaved blacks in Portuguese America. In addition, the Indians and mestizos were more resistant to the Europeans' quest for economic and political power. They were less likely to be exterminated, and more likely to be Christianized. Comprising approximately 75 percent of the population, illiterate, uneducated, provincial, and geographically and economically immobile, the Indians and mestizos were the lower half of a class system dominated by Spaniards and Creoles.

Nor was the intellectual heritage of the Spanish who dominated Latin America throughout its modern history equal to that of the English who prevailed in the formative years of the American colonies. Spanish Catholicism included elements of superstition, irrationality, and intolerance. American society, on the other hand, was highlighted by a middle class interest in expanding democracy, maintaining religious diversity, and emphasizing education and economic success as virtues for the individual. The North American war of independence also did not bequeath a military tradition like that in Latin America after 1826. Political instability, often resulting from military coups, was especially widespread in Latin America in the century following independence. Economic development, although accelerating noticeably in the late nineteenth century, was significantly retarded by revolution and warfare.

Yet, after a period of experimentation from the time of independence, the lure and reality of the presidential system remain strong in Latin America today (except in the British Commonwealth countries). Although ten countries are presently ruled by military dictatorship, they all still retain the presidential form. Ten others have presidents more analogous to the U. S. model. Six of these—Guatemala, El Salvador, Costa Rica, the Dominican Republic, Venezuela, and Colombia—are examples in which the race for the presidency is competitive. Four illustrate presidential systems of a "managed" or "controlled" nature: Mexico, Nicaragua, Brazil, and Paraguay. And throughout the continent, even among military dictators, the term "president" is widespread and revered, often as a symbol of political legitimacy.

This volume arose from a conference in the spring of 1976 on the presidential system of government. Held at the American University in Washington, D.C., the conference brought together some 50 scholars and statesmen to analyze the past, present, and future of the presidential system of government in the United States, Latin America, Africa, and Europe. The outcome of the Latin American segment of the conference has been sharpened and extended in this volume: two chapters focus on the historical evolution of the presidential system in the cultural, political, social, and economic milieux of the various countries and on the attempts to restrain presidential power. The remaining chapters focus on specific countries illustrative of presidential systems: Mexico, with a managed presidency, and Colombia, Costa Rica, and Venezuela, with electoral systems more analogous to the U. S. model. In each of the chapters the concern of the authors has been to answer questions relating to presidential power. To what extent, for example, have constitutional and extralegal determinants defined the nature of presidential power in Latin America? Is *caudillismo* or *personalismo* the subtle characteristic distinguishing one presidential system from another? Or are the interest system, party system, and degree of economic sophistication the more important determinants of presidential power? To what extent does U. S. foreign policy—both overt and covert—determine the constraints and excesses of presidential power in Latin America? What does all of this bode for the future?

I am indebted to the American University for its support of the Conference on the Presidential System of Government; to Dr. Frank Barros, the university's director of academic development and research, who masterfully handled the conference arrangements; and to Dr. Harold E. Davis, professor emeritus, and Dr. Hugo Pineda, associate professor of language and foreign studies, both of the American University, on whose expertise I relied during the conference and in editing this volume. The contributors share with me full responsibility for any errors of fact, interpretation, or propriety in the text, as well as the earnest hope that readers will leave the volume with an enlightened understanding of the historical and contemporary issues relating to presidential power in Latin America.

# CONTENTS

# Presidential Power in
# Latin American Politics

# CAUDILLOS, CORONEIS, AND
# POLITICAL BOSSES IN
# LATIN AMERICA
### Robert J. Alexander

Latin American politics is often portrayed as being dominated by "personalism." It is frequently said that political struggles are merely contests between competing leaders with more or less charisma, each with a greater or smaller band of devoted followers. As a result, this argument goes, ideas and principles play an insignificant role, parties are mere congregations of followers of one or another leader, political institutions are mere instruments to be used by whoever is in power at any given moment to further his own interests and achieve exaltation.

If this was ever a correct picture of Latin American politics, it is no longer. Political parties, differentiated from one another by more or less clear-cut principles and programs, representing fairly well-defined interests and having lives extending well beyond those of any individual leaders, have played a significant role in Latin American politics in recent decades. The military have become institutionalized, and now tend to operate as a cohesive body rather than as the coterie of a particular army chieftain. Dictatorships may continue to bend political institutions to their will and convenience, but they do so on behalf of a ruling group, not to suit the whims of a single charismatic despot.

Of course, leadership remains an important ingredient of Latin American politics, as it does of politics in any part of the world. But it is no longer the case, if it ever was, that political activity can be simply reduced to struggles for power between rival chieftains around whose personalities and persons are grouped larger or smaller segments of the active citizenry.

However, in most countries the stabilization of politics through political parties, highly disciplined military, and more or less stable institutions is a twentieth-century phenomenon. The political history of Latin America since independence has provided a number of types of personalist rule. Here, I shall discuss three of these: the *caudillo* of Spanish America, the *coronel* of Brazil, and the more modern political boss in several countries. The last of these will have certain characteristics familiar to students of U.S. history. The caudillos and the coroneis, on the other hand, are more typically Latin American phenomena, growing out of the peculiar circumstances of those countries.

## THE MEANING OF "CAUDILLO"

The word "caudillo" is sometimes freely translated as "leader." In recent decades it has taken on some of the connotations of such titles as *der Führer* and *il Duce.* Thus, Spanish coins of recent decades have proclaimed Francisco Franco to be "By Grace of God, Caudillo of Spain." A variety of other figures have been loosely called caudillos, including Juan Perón, Fidel Castro, and even Rómulo Betancourt. We shall pay some attention to their cases.

However, I am using the term "caudillo" in a more specific sense. By it, I mean a particular type of Spanish American political leader who was a characteristic figure of many of the newly-independent Spanish American countries during much of the nineteenth and the twentieth centuries.

## ORIGINS OF THE CAUDILLO

The caudillos arose in Spanish America in the aftermath of the wars of independence. They owed their origin in large part to the peculiar circumstances in which these countries found themselves once they had thrown off the yoke of the "mother country."

Under Spanish colonial rule there was little if any tradition of self-government. In contrast to the situation in the British North American colonies, there were no autonomous provincial legislatures with legitimate roles derived directly or indirectly from the king and Parliament. Government of state and Church in Spanish America was in the hands of *peninsulares,* that is, people sent from the Iberian peninsula to fill posts in the hierarchies of both the lay and clerical regimes.

Also, there was a different tradition with regard to the military in Spanish and British America. In the latter case, after the short English experience with the military dictatorship of Oliver Cromwell, the subordination of the armed forces to the civilian authority was strongly asserted, and had become a well-entrenched tradition by the time the North American colonies rebelled. In Spanish America the situation was markedly different. The military, both in Spain and in the Spanish colonies, had a special place and enjoyed privileges, the so-called *fueros militares.* These special provisions of the law removed military men from the jurisdiction of the civil courts—they could only be tried in military tribunals, where presumably they would receive more sympathetic treatment. Furthermore, members of the armed forces—whether of the regular

Spanish army or of the local militia—were exempt from certain taxes that more ordinary mortals were expected to pay.

Thus, the conditions at the time of independence militated in favor of the emergence of the military with a political role. On the one hand, there was a vacuum of legitimacy, which the new regimes sought unsuccessfully to fill. In contrast to the situation in the North American colonies, where the quite legitimate provincial legislatures merely decided to replace the king and Parliament by the Continental Congress as the highest level of the governmental hierarchy, in Spanish America the movement for independence was not undertaken by legitimately constituted authorities, but rather by ad hoc ones engendered by the act of revolution.

On the other hand, unhampered by a firmly rooted tradition of civilian supremacy over the armed forces, the military leaders of the Spanish American independence movements felt relatively little compunction about sending home the civilian legislators if they got in the way of what the military chiefs wanted to do. This stands in sharp contrast to the actions of George Washington, an Englishman to the core, who stubbornly refused to move against the Continental Congress no matter how much he and other leaders of the revolutionary army felt that they were hampering the struggle for independence.

The upshot of all of this was that the revolutionary armed forces emerged from the independence struggles as virtually the only legitimate authorities—their legitimacy based on the fact that they were the ones immediately responsible for bringing about the new state of affairs, that is, independence. Furthermore, in many instances the military leaders emerged immediately as heads of the governments and of the new states. The one remaining institution that might have asserted a degree of legitimacy, the Church, was severely hampered from doing so by the fact that it had generally sided with the Spaniards, not with the colonists, and by the additional fact that the Vatican was exceedingly tardy in recognizing the existence of most of the independent states, thus leaving the Church in Spanish America virtually without bishops.

Almost before the battles for independence had been won, however, the revolutionary armies began to disintegrate. In part this was because in much of the area they had in fact been more or less loose coalitions of military forces basically loyal to their own commanders rather than to the new national governments. Once independence was a reality, this process of disintegration was intensified, and the caudillo emerged.

## CHARACTERISTICS OF THE CAUDILLO

The caudillo was essentially a charismatic figure. His power rested on the personal loyalty of his followers to him and to his destiny. He was frequently a local landholder of some consequence who could command the obedience and loyalty of his own employees as the core of his political and military following. In some cases he undoubtedly had oratorical ability; in others he had other personal characteristics that won him the respect and loyalty of his cohorts. Thus, Juan Manuel de Rosas, the famous Argentine caudillo and a man of the pampas, was reputed to be able to ride down a cow and perform the other feats characteristic of the gaucho of his time better than virtually any of his own followers.

The typical caudillo began as a regional leader, in competition with other regional leaders. Through superior military ability, a more attractive personality, guile, or a greater capacity for political maneuvering, some caudillos were able to defeat or gain the support of rival regional leaders. If he felt that the strength of his forces justified it, a caudillo might make a descent upon the national capital and proclaim himself the president of the republic or place some puppet figure in that post. If he lacked the force for this, he would be obliged to limit his own ambitions to maintaining control over his own region and perhaps would join forces with some more powerful colleague, to place him in the presidential chair.

One must bear in mind that through much of the nineteenth century, and in some countries well into the twentieth century, armaments were relatively primitive. A leader who could command a solid band of hard-riding horsemen armed with rifles, or even in some cases with spears, represented a formidable military force when competing with other forces similarly armed.

The caudillo was thus a combination of popular folk hero, astute political leader, and military man. He ruled in a very personal way over the area under his control. If he had been sufficiently successful to become the national leader, his continuance in this post usually depended on his ability to maintain the loyalty of regional leaders similar to himself and to quash the ambitions of those who might challenge his control of the country. He often was quite willing to allow regional caudillos to rule their own areas as if these were their personal estates, so long as the regional leaders did not challenge his control of the nation as a whole.

National armies of the time were congregations of the loyal followers of the dominant caudillo. These were graduates of the hard school of caudillo military politics, rather than of the academies. A general might well be illiterate, but if he could command the loyalty of a sizable group of followers and had evidenced a certain amount of military capacity in the internecine warfare generally characteristic of these countries, he could maintain his power and the rank that went with it.

## EXAMPLES OF CAUDILLOS

One can find many examples of the caudillo in the history of Spanish America during the nineteenth and early twentieth centuries. We have already mentioned Juan Manuel de Rosas, who was only one of many similar figures who dominated Argentina during the period between independence and the end of the caudillo era in 1860. Domingo Sarmiento has immortalized one of these figures, Facundo Quiroga, in his famous book *Facundo,* which he subtitled "Civilization and Barbarism," Quiroga obviously representing the latter.

Bolivia was dominated until the War of the Pacific, begun in 1879, by a long series of caudillos, including Andrés Santa Cruz and the perversely famous Mariano Melgarejo. Uruguay was founded by caudillos and their epoch did not end until the advent to power in 1904 of José Batlle y Ordóñez.

In Venezuela, a long series of caudillos from the *llanos,* or great plains, who dominated the country after its independence, was succeeded after 1900 by caudillos who came from the mountain state of Tachira. The last of these, the notorious Juan Vicente Gómez, labelled the Tyrant of the Andes by one of his biographers, died peacefully in his sleep in December 1935. He ended *caudillismo* in Venezuela by creating a professional army.

In the Dominican Republic the age of the caudillo lasted virtually from the country's independence from Haiti in 1844 until 1930. It finally came to an end with the dictatorship of Rafael Leonidas Trujillo, which, although intensely personal and probably more complete in its tryanny than any other Latin American regime of its time, was the product of a regular army, not of caudillismo.

Caudillos dominated Mexico during most of the nineteenth century. Perhaps the most notorious figure of this kind was the ill-fated Antonio López de Santa Anna. The country was subjected to a somewhat different type of caudillismo during the intermittent civil wars which marked the decade after the outbreak of the revolution of 1910. It took nearly two more decades for successive presidents, as least some of whom were themselves caudillos, to put an end to the phenomenon in that republic. Mariano Azuela's famous novel *Los de Abajo* paints a vivid sketch of the rise and nature of the Mexican revolutionary caudillos.

Finally, caudillismo lasted longer in Central America than in any other part of Latin America. Although Costa Rica was generally not characterized by the phenomenon, neighboring Nicaragua was dominated by caudillos until the United States intervened at the time of World War I. Caudillos ruled Guatemala and El Salvador until 1944, and the last of the Honduran caudillos, Tiburcio Carías Andino, only retired voluntarily—an action quite uncharacteristic of the species—in 1948.

## THE DECLINE OF CAUDILLISMO

A number of factors combined to undermine caudillismo. One of these was the emergence of a professional military in the Latin American countries.

As Professors John Johnson and Edwin Lieuwen have indicated in their well-known studies of the Latin American military, this process began in some countries in the last decades of the nineteenth century, whereas it took place only several decades later in the smaller countries of the area.

Military academies were established, often by military missions from Germany or France. These turned out a different kind of young officer from those characteristic of the caudillo armies. The graduates of the military academies were imbued with a vision of themselves as leaders of the most important national institution, the loyalty of which was to the fatherland rather than to any particular political leader. A strong sense of esprit de corps was instilled in them, and they came to conceive of themselves as having a special responsibility for the welfare of the nation. Furthermore, many of the academy graduates—particularly in such army branches as the artillery, communications, and engineering—emerged with a degree of technical training and sophistication which reinforced their conviction that they were an elite group.

Changes in the military technology in the last decades of the nineteenth century and during the twentieth also served to undermine the caudillo. The introduction of machine guns, sophisticated artillery, and, somewhat later, tanks and airplanes upset the balance of the military power upon which the rule of the caudillo had been based. A group of horsemen armed with more or less primitive rifles or spears was no longer capable of challenging effectively the national army. The traditional descent upon the captial by an armed band behind an aspiring caudillo-president became a thing of the past.

Economic changes beginning in the second half of the nineteenth century also contributed substantially to making the caudillo an anachronism. The growth of export industries based on the products of modern plantation agriculture or modern mining was accompanied by the expansion of transportation systems, first railroads and later highways. The same phenomenon provoked a substantial increase in the size, economic activity, and political power and influence of the cities. The national government was called upon to play an increasingly important economic and social role, thus strengthening its power vis-a-vis local and regional leaders.

These trends were intensified as the region began to industrialize seriously during and after World War I. New working classes and a variety of middle groups in the cities, on the railroads, on the plantations, in the mines, and in government and private offices began to be increasingly vociferous in making demands upon the state and the economy. Social and economic issues became more important than the personal charisma of individual political leaders.

The upshot of this was the disappearance of the caudillo even in the smaller countries of Latin America by the middle of the twentieth century. Although this did not mean the universalization of political democracy and interest group politics in the area, it did mean that regimes of force, which remained prevalent, were no longer based on the caudillo. Dictatorships were installed by the military as an institution, rather than by bands of armed followers of a particular political chieftain. Any particular dictator—or any democratically elected president—could only remain in power so long as he had the support of the top echelon of the military bureaucracy.

## CAUDILLOS VERSUS CONTEMPORARY MILITARY DICTATORSHIPS

Contemporary military regimes differ profoundly from those of the caudillos. A few examples of these differences will suffice.

The thinly veiled military dictatorship that has ruled Brazil since 1964, for example, has been a highly institutionalized regime. The movement that brought the military to power was carried out by most of the officer corps as a group. They chose the commander in chief of the army, Marshal Humberto Castelo Branco, as their first president. He was succeeded by the minister of war of the outgoing chief executive. When this successor, Marshal Arthur Costa e Silva, died, a poll of the principal military officers resulted in the selection of the relatively obscure General Emílio Garrastazú Médici, who in turn was succeeded in a "constitutional" process by the present president, General Ernesto Geisel.

None of these men has had the characteristics of a caudillo. Each was selected by the leadership of the armed forces as a whole. None has had anything like absolute personal power while in the presidency, each in turn having been subject to conflicting pressures from within the military and having seen his program largely frustrated by these pressures. In sum, the military dictatorship of Brazil in the last dozen years has been a dictatorship exercised by the armed forces as an institution—or a conglomeration of institutions.

Much the same has been true of the military regime which has been in power in Peru since 1968. There, too, the movement that overthrew the democratically elected civilian regime of President Fernando Belaunde Terry was carried out under the direction of the top leadership of the three armed forces. The chief of the strongest of these, the army, more or less automatically took over as president. In 1975, however, when General Juan Velasco displeased the principal figures of the military, he was deposed, and the next-ranking army general took his place in the presidency. Although there have been conflicting currents of opinion within the armed forces, the programs of reform carried out by the Peruvian regime have been the work of the top military leadership as a group, not those of any particular charismatic figure among them.

Likewise, since 1973 the Chilean government has been in the hands of the top officers of the four armed forces—army, navy, air force, and militarized police, or *carabineros*—who had taken the leadership of the movement to oust President Salvador Allende. The army, as the strongest of the four groups, provided the titular leadership, in the person of General Pinochet. He has, however, occupied that post as a representative of his military arm, not because of any personal attributes. The policies of the regime have been determined by the ranking officials of the armed services and do not represent the personal will of the president or any other single member of the ruling junta.

Many similar examples could be cited to demonstrate that there is a profound difference between the institutionalized military dictatorships of the latter part of the twentieth century and the caudillo regimes of the first hundred years or so of the independence of the Latin American countries.

## CAUDILLOS VERSUS POPULIST LEADERS

To clarify the historical role of the caudillo it is worthwhile to compare him not only with the present-day military dictator, but also with the twentieth-century populist political leader. The word "caudillo" has frequently been used rather loosely to describe some populist politicians.

The populist, like the caudillo, is a person with considerable popular support. The populist, however, unlike the traditional caudillo, usually represents or favors particular interest groups in his national society and derives his popular support from this fact. The populist also does not depend for his success on the kind of nonprofessional military cohorts who were essential to the caudillo.

To differentiate the caudillo more clearly from the recent populist politician, it will be useful to look at specific cases of populist political leaders from recent Latin American history. For this purpose, Getúlio Vargas, Juan Perón, Rómulo Betancourt, and Fidel Castro will be useful.

Getúlio Vargas was undoubtedly the most popular Brazilian political figure of the twentieth century. He originally came to power as the result of a revolt in which the military police of several states and a dissident element of the federal army triumphed over that part of the federal armed forces which remained loyal to the deposed government. Upon assuming office as provisional president, Vargas was virtually a prisoner of the military who had put him in power. To gain himself freedom of action vis-a-vis the institutionalized military, Vargas did two things: he split the military leaders and restored the armed forces' discipline and hierarchy, and he built up a large civilian constituency by fostering the unionization—under state control—of urban workers and by enacting extensive legislation on their behalf. He succeeded. From 1933 until 1945, his regime rested on the support of the army and of the urban workers, recruiting as well the backing of most of the rapidly expanding industrialist class.

Vargas was overthrown by the military in 1945, and for the remaining nine years of his life, although he continued to have the loyalty of a majority of the working class, he was regarded at best with skepticism by the military hierarchy. It was the military who, by threatening to overthrow him for a second time after his reelection in 1950, drove Vargas to suicide in August 1954.

Although Vargas had the kind of personal devotion from his followers which had been enjoyed by the caudillos, this support was not based on the attraction of his personality or his individual valor, but rather on the fact that he had done much for the workers and the industrialists—or at least they were convinced that he had. Furthermore, their support was civil, not military; these backers were never organized militarily to seize or hold power. The only military backing Vargas received came from the institutionalized armed forces, but the army, navy, and air force of Brazil were never in any sense the personal armed forces of Getúlio Vargas.

Juan Perón was himself a professional army officer, who began his rise to power when the military as a body deposed a civilian president. He got the upper hand politically over his fellow officers by mobilizing the working class on his behalf. As in the case of Vargas, Perón won this working class support by encouraging the spread of the trade union movement and by enacting a great deal of labor legislation.

Throughout his first period in power, Perón's regime was based on the twin forces of the labor movement and the armed forces. During the 18 years between his overthrow and his return to power, he was kept out of office by the military, although he continued to have the backing of a majority of the organized workers. He was finally allowed to come back to power when the military chiefs became convinced that they had failed in their efforts to run the country and that Perón had the support not only of the trade union movement but of the great majority of the Argentine civilians.

As in the case of Vargas, Perón's popular support was based on the self-interest of his supporters rather than on Perón's personal charisma or valor—indeed, he was widely reputed to be a coward. Also, like Vargas, it was the institutionalized armed forces that both helped him get to power and overthrew him. He never had at his service a military whose basic loyalty was to him rather than to the armed forces as an institution and to Argentina as a nation. Thus, Perón was no more a caudillo than was Vargas.

Rómulo Betancourt has undoubtedly been the most important political leader of Venezuela in this century. He has sometimes referred to himself as a caudillo, particularly during and just after his second period in the presidency, in the early 1960s. Betancourt, however, was no more a real caudillo than were Vargas and Perón. His strength in politics came from his ability to organize and lead a civilian political party with a well-defined ideology and program. Through this party large elements of the urban working class and the peasantry were organized for political purposes. During its several periods in power, the party served the interests of these social groups, consolidating its support among them.

In the case of Betancourt it was his ideas and his capacity as a practical politician, as well as his loyalty to the party and its programs and to his fellow party leaders, which won and kept for him the support of his fellow citizens. The attitude of the institutionalized armed forces toward him varied at different times. In all phases of his career, however, Betancourt was dealing with an army, navy, and air force, each with a marked sense of its own importance and viewing itself as loyal to the Venezuelan nation, not to any particular political leader.

Finally, there is Fidel Castro. He comes closer than the other three political leaders to being a caudillo. He did come to power due at least in part to the efforts of an irregular rebel army loyal to him. Castro had great personal charisma. The loyalty of his followers was to his personality rather than to any ideas or programs, since he changed these several times during his rise to and exercise of power. In the first years after Castro's advent to power, the armed forces consisted of troops whose principal loyalty was to him; all officers whose loyalty was doubtful were purged.

Thus, on his road to power and for some time thereafter Castro had many of the characteristics of the caudillo. Castro later institutionalized his regime, however, partly through his own initiative and partly because he was forced into it. Through the organization of the Communist party, the establishment of a conscript army, the universalization of the secret police, and the establishment of a variety of mass organizations, the Cuban regime was transformed from a caudillo-led one into a Communist government in the Soviet mold. Indeed, Soviet influence was a major factor in bringing about this transformation.

## ORIGINS OF THE CORONEL

Like the caudillo of Spanish America, the *coronel,* or "colonel," of Brazil emerged as a result of the decay of existing institutions. His origins, however, were substantially different from those of the caudillo.

The title "colonel" in the Brazilian context has some of the attributes of the Kentucky colonel in the United States. It does not indicate that the individual involved was an officer of a duly constituted armed force. On the other hand, as we shall see, the Brazilian colonel had considerably more power than his Kentucky counterpart.

Brazil was not characterized by the caudillo because Brazilian independence was achieved under quite different circumstances from those in the former Spanish colonies. The scion of the Portuguese royal family, Dom Pedro, who had been left as regent in Brazil by his father, King João VI, took the initiative in proclaiming the independence of the country. The military struggle to expel those Portuguese troops who would not go along with the new order lasted only about a year, so that the new Brazilian army did not assume the proportions of its counterparts in Spanish America. Nor did the military forces supporting the newly independent government of Brazil degenerate into bands of personal followers of political leaders, as in the Spanish American countries, since the Brazilian army was defending a monarch who was generally seen as legitimate.

In Brazil, therefore, there was no vacuum of legitimacy, with the heir to the throne succeeding to it, and the Catholic Church almost immediately recognizing Brazilian independence. The Brazilian army remained small and relatively weak: indeed, as General Nelson Werneck Sodre and other historians of the Brazilian armed forces have pointed out, it became the deliberate policy of the imperial government to keep the army in a secondary role. This policy only changed when Brazil became involved in the long and costly War of the Triple Alliance with Paraguay, from 1865 to 1870.

Thus, the Brazilian armed forces never disintegrated into caudillo-led bands. When, after the War of the Triple Alliance, and even more so after the proclamation of the republic in 1889, the military began to play a political role, it did so as an institution, not as a collection of forces loyal to local caudillos. *Coronelismo* thus had different origins from those of caudillismo. It was a phenomenon of the so-called Old Republic of 1889 to 1930. The coronel became a key political figure because of the disintegration of the plantation system of colonial and imperial Brazil, and because of the dismantling of the political structure that had predominated during the Empire.

The large, slave-worked plantation had dominated colonial Brazil and was preponderant in most of the country even during the Empire. This was particularly the case in the Northeast, where the coronel was most prevalent. The traditional plantation was in many ways self-sufficient: the plantation not only produced a crop for export, such as sugar or cacao, but also grew most of the food for the slaves and the "big house." The houses of the masters and the shanties of the slaves were built by the slaves, who also made much, if not most, of the clothing they used.

Furthermore, the owner of the plantation and the slaves was the master of the land and all the people on it. He administered what justice there was to his dependents and slaves; he was responsible for the church building and the priest who served it. He organized and sometimes led the militia, generally officered by plantation owners or their sons, with free or subordinate whites serving as noncommissioned officers and slaves serving as rank-and-file soldiers. This body kept order and performed police functions in the areas dominated by large plantations.

The autonomy of the plantation had begun to deterioriate even in the colonial period, and this disintegration continued during the Empire. To an increasing degree the plantation owner came to need services from the government of the locality or the province. For its part, the government, at various levels, sought bit-by-bit to increase its influence over the hinterland, and thus over the plantation. By the time of the fall of the Empire in 1889 the situation had developed sufficiently so there was a role for the coronel. This role was the more necessary because of sweeping changes in governmental organizations brought about by the inauguration of the republic.

Under the Empire, the provincial governors, or *"presidentes,"* as they were called, were appointed by the national government. They in turn appointed the local representatives of governmental authority in the municipalities. Thus, neither state nor local officials were dependent directly on the support or goodwill of local landholders to gain office or to hold onto it.

The political organization of the Old Republic was markedly different from that of the Empire. The states were given a wide degree of autonomy, to the point of being able to raise customs duties against goods brought in from other units of the federation. Furthermore, state governors were elected rather than appointed by the national government. Similarly, municipal executives were elected instead of being named by the state governors.

## CHARACTERISTICS OF THE CORONEL

This situation created the circumstances for the emergence of the coronel, who was an intermediary between the local landlords and the state government. He obtained from the state government favors and local improvements desired by the landlords within his jurisdiction, in return for their votes in local, state, and federal elections. On the other hand, the coroneis were the cornerstones of the "Republican parties" that supported the government of most of the states during the period of the Old Republic. These parties were loose coalitions of the local machines of the coroneis, and the governor, in order to maintain control, needed the support of the coroneis in his state.

The military situation in the Old Republic also reinforced the importance of the coroneis. The federal army remained comparatively small and weak, and the states had their own militarized state police. In the larger states, in particular, these state police were more numerous and at least as well armed as the federal army units stationed there.

The state police maintained "law and order" in the states. Their support was not only important for the maintenance of state power, but also occasionally of great significance to the coroneis. When, as happened sometimes, coroneis were faced with opposition in their territories, it was important to have the governor send state police units to buttress their rule, to permit the coroneis to count ballots as they saw fit, and perhaps to remove the opposition leaders as "trouble makers." Jorge Amado and José Guimaraes Rosa have described this in some of their novels.

Another aspect of the role of the coronel, particularly in the Northeast, was his relationship with the *cangaceiro*. The cangaceiro was really an outlaw. He headed a group of armed men who razed plantations, small town businesses and banks, and other enterprises. Often a leader of the opposition to local coroneis he was sometimes their ally, reinforcing the coroneis' control. Indeed, sometimes the line between a coronel and a cangaceiro was shadowy.

The federal government had many similarities to the state regimes in this period. As the state administration depended on the local coroneis, the federal government depended on the backing of the various state Republican parties. Thus, the coroneis were the cornerstone of not only the state but also the federal government during the Old Republic.

The nature of the regime was shown by the virtual unanimity that characterized federal elections during the Old Republic. Only one presidential election was seriously contested during this period, that of 1910, when the issue of militarism was injected into the contest and the state Republican parties divided between the official candidate, Marshal Hermes Fonseca, and the opposition, antimilitarist nominee, Ruy Barbosa.

Similarly, real election contests only took place on the state level when there was division among the coroneis. Such contests did appear from time to time in Baia, Ceará, and other states. Only in the state of Río Grande do Sul was the ruling Republican party constantly faced with a strong opposition, the Federal party, which had its own coroneis and sometimes resorted to armed insurrection against the state government. During the last decade of the Old Republic, opposition Democratic parties appeared in several states, notably São Paulo, but they did not represent a major challenge to the Republican parties' control.

The nature of the political situation was well illustrated by the election of 1930, a few months before the end of the Old Republic. The government candidate for president was Júlio Prestes, governor of São Paulo. His opponent was Governor Getúlio Vargas of Río Grande do Sul, who had Governor João Pessôa of the state of Paraíba as his vice-presidential nominee: they were supported by the Republican party machine of Minas Gerais. The opposition won only in the states of Río Grande do Sul, Paraíba, and Minas Gerais, where they obtained almost all of the votes; the government won in all of the rest of the states, also nearly unanimously.

## THE DECLINE OF THE CORONEL

The role of the coronel declined sharply with the advent of the revolution of 1930 and the New Republic. The reasons for this decline were somewhat similar to those which brought about the demise of the caudillo in Spanish America.

The government of President Getúlio Vargas, which remained in office in one form or another for 15 years, effectively broke down the autonomy of the Brazilian states. For more than three years after the revolution of October 1930, the states were ruled by interventors, appointed by the president of the republic, who appointed local mayors. Although the constitution of 1934 restored a wide degree of self-government to the states, it was suspended by President Vargas when he made the coup of November 10, 1937 and established the *Estado Novo* or "New State." For a decade after that, the states were again ruled by federally appointed interventors, and the municipalities by appointed mayors.

There were also no elections, except for the short period when the 1934 constitution was in force. Thus, the intermediary role of the coronel as mobilizer of votes for the state administration, in return for favors for his constituents and himself, was no longer necessary.

Furthermore, the balance of military power within the republic shifted during the Vargas regime. The federal army was much strengthened, while the state police were reduced in numbers and armament and were placed under the control of army officers. A determined effort was made to suppress the cangaceiros, and by the end of the Estado Novo they were a thing of the past.

The economic development fostered by the Vargas regime, which stimulated industrialization, also undermined the position of the coronel. In addition, many new roads were built, which, although generally not paved, tended to reduce substantially the isolation of large areas of the country. Much of the power of the coronel had been based on his control of relatively isolated parts of the country.

Yet the coronel had by no means disappeared by the end of the Vargas dictatorship. When a more or less democratic regime was reestablished after 1945, and elections again became the order of the day, the states regained a substantial part of their autonomy. Thus, there was once again a role for intermediaries between local economic and political interests and the state governments. Furthermore, the Vargas regime had not actually tried to destroy the coronel as a political actor; if coroneis were loyal to Vargas, they were allowed to retain whatever local power they could muster. The role of these intermediaries, however, was considerably different after 1945 from what it had been before 1930. The regional political chief was much more akin to a political boss than to a coronel during the democratic interlude of 1945–64.

With the reestablishment of a dictatorial regime after the coup of April 1, 1964, there was little room for the coronel. The military regime had no place in its organization for such independent bases of power as the coroneis' fiefs represented. One can now say, probably, that the traditional coronel has passed into history.

## POLITICAL BOSSISM IN LATIN AMERICA

Political bossism, as we have been accustomed to in the United States, has not been as prevalent in Latin America. There have, however, been examples of this kind of political phenomenon.

It is useful to define bossism and differentiate it from caudillismo and coronelismo. Bossism can be said to be a system, the principal characteristics of which are organization and patronage. It differs from caudillismo in that it does not depend upon the personal charisma of any particular leader. It differs from coronelismo in that the bosses' machines do not have the intermediary position that the coronel had between higher and lower levels of government; instead, the machine tends to encompass several levels of administration.

Bossism is characteristic of a system in which regimes are chosen (at least formally) by elections. The principal function of the bosses is to organize the voters, see that they get to the polls, and assure that the votes are counted favorably.

### The PRI As a System of Political Bossism

Perhaps the most outstanding and long-lasting example of political bossism in Latin America is the government party of Mexico, the *Partido Revolucionario Institucional* (PRI). This is the political organization that has dominated Mexico since 1929.

The PRI, first called the *Partido Nacional Revolucionario,* rose to the control of political life in the wake of the decline of the caudillos of the Mexican Revolution. Ex-President Plutarco Elías Calles, the founder of the PRI, consciously established the party as a means of curbing the still prevalent caudillos. He endowed it, from the beginning, with a substantial income by making all government employees pay contributions to it. Increasingly, he brought under the control of the party those public jobs subject to political appointment.

President Lázaro Cárdenas modified the form of organization of the party and reinforced its patronage powers and ability to mobilize voters. He converted it into a collegiate party, to which many of the country's key interest groups were directly affiliated. He thus mobilized the structures of the labor movement, the major peasant group, and a variety of middle class organizations to carry on the party's work.

For many decades the PRI has counted on patronage as a key to its power. The top national party leaders have at their disposal not only political jobs in the administrative side of the government, but also the party's legislative posts, which are allotted in return for party loyalty. On lower governmental levels, the PRI state governors have similar patronage powers at their command within their jurisdictions.

There are, of course, elements other than patronage in the Mexican political picture. One of these is the ability of the government and PRI leaders to count ballots on all levels. Few people would be so rash as to maintain that ballots in Mexico are always—or even usually—counted as they are actually cast. This discrepancy is perhaps a characteristic of bossism, however; certainly it was not alien to Tammany Hall in its heyday.

The Mexican system certainly does not involve the charisma which was such an integral part of caudillismo. Most recent Mexican presidents have not been charismatic figures. Their power derives from their position at the head of the PRI machine, not from their ability to arouse widespread personal loyalty from their followers.

Nor do the PRI politicians have the intermediary role of the Brazilian coronel. For, while they are parts of a nationally integrated machine that does seek to mediate the interests of a variety of interest groups in the society, they are not clearly middle men between any two specific levels of government.

The role of the Mexican president within this system is unique. It has become traditional that during the six years that he is the chief executive he is immune from open personal attack. His subordinates may be criticized in the press and elsewhere, but not the president himself. Some wit has remarked that the president of Mexico is "an absolute monarch with a six year term of office," which, at least in terms of his immunity from attack, is not far from the mark. Furthermore, the Mexican president has exceedingly extensive power, having the last word in selecting the leadership of the government party, the governors of states, and the members of Congress. However, in all of these matters, as well as in the selection of his successor, the president is expected to play within certain well-recognized rules of the game. These rules are elastic and subject to varying interpretation, but undoubtedly a president who would operate clearly outside of them would provoke a major constitutional crisis.

In spite of his immunity from criticism and his wide powers, however, the Mexican president is not a caudillo. These attributes are not personal to him —he loses them the moment he ceases to be president—but are associated with the office of president. It is not his personal charisma or popularity that gives him power, but rather the institutionalization of the post that he holds.

## Chilean Bossism in the Parliamentary Republic

A much earlier example of bossism in Latin American politics was the situation in Chile during the period of the parliamentary republic, from 1891 to 1924. During this period most provinces were dominated by machines, whose functions were to mobilize and count the votes and to dispense patronage to the faithful.

Two factors reinforced the boss system in Chile. One was the electoral procedure, which allowed votes to be cast in absentia: the boss collected as many voting certificates as possible from the local electors and cast them all for the candidates of his choice. The second factor favoring the boss system was the parliamentary form of government. The provincial boss was usually a member of the Senate or Chamber of Deputies. There he belonged to one of the many parties or party factions that made the Chilean parliamentary system reminiscent of that of Third and Fourth Republic France. The number of these groups, and the unreliability of discipline within most of them, led to rapid turnover of cabinets.

It became the accepted practice for a provincial boss who wanted to have a supporter appointed to a local judgeship, tax collector's post, or mayor's position, or who wanted to get some public works project for his constituency, to present such a demand to the president. If the chief executive showed hesitation, the boss would threaten to join the opposition, push through a vote of no confidence in one or the other house of the parliament, and thus bring down the incumbent cabinet. When a cabinet fell, which usually occurred every few months, the constitution of a new one presented additional opportunities for the bosses to present their patronage demands to the president as the price for their support of the new group of ministers.

These Chilean political bosses would often control a province for a whole generation. This was the case with the machine of Senator Arturo del Río of Tarapaca, who dominated that province virtually from the time it was acquired by Chile in the 1879 War of the Pacific until he was finally defeated in the parliamentary election of 1916.

This election illustrates the system well. Senator del Río not only mobilized the voters to confront his challenger, Arturo Alessandri, but also used outright intimidation, including attempts to assassinate the rival candidate. Del Río's machine was only defeated as a result of Alessandri's ability to convince the president of the republic to send military units to the province to maintain order and to preside over the counting of the ballots. Alessandri's success in defeating an entrenched political boss was such an extraordinary occurrence that it immediately catapulted a hitherto somewhat run-of-the-mill deputy into the leading candidate for the presidency of the republic.

## The PSD of Minas

A third outstanding example of bossism is to be found in Brazil during the democratic period period of 1945–64. To greater or less degrees, the three major parties of that period—the *Partido Social Democrático* (PSD), *União Democrática Nacional* (UDN), and *Partido Trabalhista Brasileiro* (PTB)— were all characterized by political bossism. The case par excellence of this kind of organization, however, was the PSD of the state of Minas Gerais, the famous *PSD de Minas.*

The principal Brazilian parties of the 1945–64 period were generally not marked by strong ideological dogma. The major factor dividing the PSD and PTB, on the one hand, from the UDN, on the other, was the fact that the first two had favored Getúlio Vargas while he was alive and honored his memory after his death, while the UDN was strongly anti-Vargas before and after his death in 1954.

The PSD of Minas was one of the strongholds of the national PSD. It controlled the state government most of the time from the end of the Estado Novo to the military coup of April 1964. It provided one president of the republic during this period, Juscelino Kubitschek, who ruled the country between 1956 and 1961.

The PSD of Minas was famous for the thoroughness of its party organization throughout Minas Gerais. The party had a local unit in virtually every population center in the state. These organizations were kept together in large part through patronage from the state government, or even the federal regime, in which the PSD was represented during most of its existence. Unlike the PRI of Mexico, the PSD of Minas depended primarily on such organization and patronage, rather than assured control of the state, to buttress its situation. Except perhaps in a few municipalities, the PSD was always subject to effective opposition from the UDN and other parties and could not manipulate election returns.

The Minas PSD was famous during its heyday for the cohesiveness of its leadership and the astuteness of its dominant group in maneuvering and bargaining with the federal government, and even with unfriendly state administrations. Its ability to funnel patronage to its party faithful was almost legendary.

Although the PSD of Minas had its roots in part in the state Republican party of the Old Republic period, it was a boss-run organization, not a phenomenon of coronelismo. It was an integrated state machine, the effectiveness of which depended basically upon organization and patronage rather than vote frauds, coercion, or (least of all) charismatic leadership.


## CONCLUSION

In this chapter I have tried to present some of the characteristics of three kinds of political organization that have dominated the political history of many of the countries in Latin America during the 150 years or more since the area achieved independence from European colonialism. Of course, there have been other kinds of authoritarian political organization in Latin America. The military dictatorship, in which the armed forces hierarchy seizes power, is perhaps the most widespread type of government today. In Cuba, there exists the only clear case of a Marxist-Leninist political model.

The three cases we have discussed, however, cover many of the political leaders and regimes that have ruled the Latin American countries since the years of independence. An understanding of them should contribute to an understanding of politics in Latin America.


## BIBLIOGRAPHICAL NOTES

So far as I know, no other attempt has been made to compare the caudillos, the coroneis, and the political bosses of Latin America. A good deal has been written about these three different types of political leaders of the area, however. I shall list here a few works that might be of interest to anyone who would like to explore further the questions I have raised in this paper.

Professors John J. Johnson, in *The Military and Society in Latin America* (Palo Alto, Calif.: Stanford University Press, 1964), and Edwin Lieuwen, in *Arms and Politics in Latin America* (New York: Praeger, 1960) have both dealt at length with the transformation of the caudillo armies into regular armies. Victor Alba, in his chapter on "Latin-American Militarism" in the volume edited by John J. Johnson, *The Role of the Military in Underdeveloped Countries* (Princeton: Princeton University Press, 1962), has also dealt with this theme.

There have been a considerable number of studies of individual caudillos. Probably the most famous of these is Domingo Faustino Sarmiento's *Facundo* (Buenos Aires: Espasa-Calpe Argentina, 1959). The last of the Venezuelan caudillos, Juan Vincente Gómez, has frequently been written about, the most famous study of him in English being Thomas Rourke's *Gómez: Tyrant of the Andes* (Garden City, N.Y.: Halcyon House, 1936). John Martz has dealt with several of the later-day Central American caudillos in his first book, *Central*

*America: The Crisis and the Challenge* (Chapel Hill: University of North Carolina Press, 1959). The famous novel by Mariano Azuela, *Los de Abajo* (Mexico City: Robredo, 1938), sketched in fictional form the rise of one of the caudillos of the Mexican revolutionary period.

One concerned with the comparison and contrast between the caudillos and the so-called populist politicians of the last couple of generations might look at my own *Prophets of the Revolution* (New York: Macmillan, 1962), which contains biographical sketches of those mentioned in this paper, as well as of several others. There are also biographies or political analyses of Perón, Getúlio Vargas, and Fidel Castro too numerous to mention.

The Brazilian coronel has received rather less attention. An important study of the coronel in decline, however, is the book of Marcos Vinicius Vilaca and Roberto C. de Albuquerque, *Coronel, Coroneis* (Rio de Janeiro: Tempo Brasileiro, 1965).

At least two sources are available that describe in some detail how the political bosses of Chile worked during the parliamentary period. One of these is the first volume of the memoirs of Arturo Alessandri Palma, *Recuerdos de gobierno* (Santiago: Editorial Nascimento, 1967), and the other is the first volume of the memoirs of Arturo Olavarria Bravo, *Chile entre dos Alessandri* (Santiago: Editorial Nascimento, 1962). Unfortunately, the best source of all, Arturo Alessandri's *Recuerdos de juventud*, got no further than page proof before the death of its editor, Guillermo Feliu Cruz, and the political upheaval of September 1973, which has severely curtailed book publishing in Chile.

There is no thorough study extant of the operations of the PSD of Minas. However, an interested reader can find out something about its role in the 1945–64 period in Thomas Skidmore's excellent study, *Politics in Brazil 1930–64: An Experiment in Democracy* (New York: Oxford University Press, 1967).

Finally, the classical source on the evolution and functioning of political bossism in Mexico of recent decades is still Robert Scott's *Mexican Government in Transition* (Urbana: University of Illinois Press, 1959).

# 2

## EFFORTS MADE BY VARIOUS LATIN AMERICAN COUNTRIES TO LIMIT THE POWER OF THE PRESIDENT
### Harry Kantor

## THE RISE OF THE ALL-POWERFUL PRESIDENT

When independence came to Latin America there was no group prepared to exercise self-government. Three hundred years of absolute monarchy, a semifeudal land tenure system, and the character of the population had not trained anyone in the art of creating or operating governmental machinery. Probably most harmful for the future development of the newly emerged independent states was the Spanish practice of filling the most important offices in the colony with appointees sent from Spain, most of whom returned to Spain after their term in office was completed. Thus, with the advent of independence there was no pool of trained administrators available to become the new government officials, nor were there any political parties, trade unions, or other social organizations whose leadership might have become the new political leaders. Some scholars have written about the *cabildo* as a form of local government that produced political leaders, but the powers of the cabildo were severely limited and were more legislative than executive.

Thus, it was logical for the victorious military leaders to turn toward the U.S. model in setting up their new governments. Many of the new leaders had lived in France and the United States. Some had fought in the French army, and many were admirers of Jefferson, Washington, and other leaders of the new United States. The leaders of the victorious armies in the new Latin American republics seemed to see the need for a strong executive around which they could unite the varied population in their new republics; yet they wanted to check the power of the new presidents, so they took the U.S. system of checks and balances as their model. They thought they would thus have what they were seeking, a strong executive limited by the power of the other branches of government.

Of course, there were some leaders who understood that a pattern of political organization cannot be transmitted from one culture to another and recommended that monarchy be continued in the newly independent states. Some of them even sent missions to Europe seeking members of various royal families willing to come to America to assume the throne, but none of these efforts was successful. Looking back we see that political behavior indeed cannot readily be transmitted from one culture to another, and that where this has been done it took a very long time before anything like success was apparent.

To put it another way, independence destroyed the only symbol of legitimacy the people knew, the crown, and substituted for it a constitutional system no one really understood. The new presidents and members of the legislatures did not have the faintest idea how to manipulate the complicated system of checks and balances, separation of powers, federalism (where this was adopted), or the other ideas contained in the U.S. Constitution created at Philadelphia. As Lord Bryce once put it in *Modern Democracies:*

> Do not give to a people institutions for which it is unripe in the simple faith that the tool will give skill to the workman's hand. Respect facts. Man is in each country not what we may wish him to be, but what nature and history have made him.*

Since the constitutional system did not work, the new republics entered a period called by most writers the "age of the *caudillos.*" The caudillos were a special type of dictator that developed out of the aristocratic and authoritarian traditions characteristic of the colonial period. They had their roots in feudal Spain and certain patterns in the Aztec and Inca empires. From independence until today the caudillo has been the typical Latin American political leader. Commander in Chief Fidel Castro, who is also first secretary of the Central Committee of the Communist party and prime minister of the revolutionary government of Cuba, and General Alfredo Stroessner, president of Paraguay since the early 1950s, exemplify two versions of the typical Latin American caudillo—the strong man, the psychological type so similar to the absolute monarch of classical Spain and the Inca and Aztec empires. Castro and Stroessner are men of superior energy and personal drive who completely dominate the governments they head. All through the period since independence such leaders have been the presidents and dictators of the various republics. Many came to power supported by the guns of their followers; others through elections. Whichever way it was, once in power as chief executives they governed as they saw fit.

---

*James Bryce, *Modern Democracies,* vol. 1 (New York: Macmillan, 1927), p. 206.

## EFFORTS TO LIMIT PRESIDENTIAL POWER

Even while the strong executive ran the governments, there always was a current of opposition to the all-powerful executive, and the large number of constitutions adopted by all of the Latin American states is eloquent testimony to the repeated efforts made to limit him. Whether this has been done effectively in any of the Latin American republics is debatable, but there is no doubt that efforts have been made. This paper is an attempt to describe and evaluate the efforts made by various Latin American countries to limit the power of their chief executives.

It can be said that talking about limits upon the chief executive in Latin America is an exercise in futility, but it is important to note that the turbulence of Latin American politics is directly related to the efforts that have been made, and are continuously being made, to limit his power. Eventually they all leave office because their term has expired or because they are overthrown or die, and new constitutions are written that include new schemes intended to truly limit presidential power. Today, ten of the Latin American republics have military dictatorships, four have presidents produced by managed elections, and only six have presidents elected in more or less competitive elections. Yet all of the countries have constitutions which prescribe all kinds of limitations upon the powers of the president.*

## No-Reelection

The most successful check upon the presidents has proved to be the denial of immediate reelection. During the past century the practice of *continuismo* was so prevalent that "no-reelection" became the slogan of the Mexican Revolution and was adopted in almost all of the other republics. By now it is part of most of the constitutions that there is no reelection, and where reelection is permitted, it is usually allowed only after one or two intervening terms. While this does not limit the president during his term of office, it puts a time limit upon how long he remains in office. At present only Paraguay and the Dominican Republic permit immediate reelection. Another such mechanism is the long list of relatives of the president and other government officials who are not allowed to run for president. Both of these schemes are infractions upon true democracy, which demands that voters be allowed to vote for

---

*The military dictatorships are Honduras, Panama, Cuba, Haiti, Argentina, Ecuador, Peru, Bolivia, Chile, and Uruguay. The presidents elected in managed elections are in Mexico, Nicaragua, Brazil, and Paraguay. The elected presidents are in Guatemala, El Salvador, Costa Rica, the Dominican Republic, Venezuela, and Colombia.

whomever they choose, yet no-reelection is a widely held opinion, and does seem to keep power limited in time.

## The Uruguayan Plural Executive

The first really well-thought-out scheme for limiting the power of the president came in Uruguay. There José Batlle y Ordóñez, one of the most remarkable political leaders Latin America has produced, came to power in the first years of the twentieth century. He was a typical caudillo, but he also was a deep political thinker. He thought that all of Uruguay's problems were rooted in the excessive power the country's constitution gave to the president. At that time, the Uruguayan president dominated the legislature and the Supreme Court during his term of office, and then selected a successor, whom he installed in office after a managed election. All that the opposition could do was accept the situation or revolt after the new president was installed. Batlle y Ordóñez decided that the cycle of revolutions, disorder, managed elections, and virtual dictatorship could be ended if the president were stripped of his power. The solution Batlle came up with was the substitution of a plural executive for a president as the chief executive.

Uruguay has twice experimented with the plural executive. The 1919 constitution divided the powers of the president into political affairs and nonpolitical affairs. The president, elected for a four-year term, retained management of foreign affairs, national defense, agriculture, and certain other matters. A nine-member national council of administration, serving a six-year term (with three members elected every two years) controlled the administration of education, health, public works, industrial relations, and the preparation of the budget. Further complicating the system, the political party receiving the second highest vote received one-third of the membership of the council. While this system brought the country's two largest political parties into the government and prevented the president from controlling all of the executive departments, it split the administration in such a way that its functioning was poor when crisis struck. When the world depression of the 1930s affected Uruguay, the system broke down and the president used his control of the armed forces to establish a dictatorship in 1933. The plural executive disappeared with the abrogation of the 1919 constitution.

The strong president either elected or in power by a coup d'etat remained the rule in Uruguay until the president elected in 1950 decided that the terrific competition during presidential election campaigns was harmful to Uruguay. He succeeded in having a constitution containing a plural executive adopted in a referendum, and in 1952 the nine-member National Council of Government became Uruguay's executive. This was a true plural executive, for none of the nine members of the council headed the executive departments, each of which was led by a minister appointed by the national council. As in the previous effort, the minority party was given one-third of the seats and the minority faction of the majority party was given one seat. As the system worked, the nine men exercised the powers normally given to a president in a presidential system, with a majority vote needed for decisions.

This was a very interesting experiment. Unfortunately, the experiment failed, probably because the National party won control of the majority of the executive council in 1959. This was the first time the National party had come to power in 93 years. It was so accustomed to being an opposition that chaos and indecision marked its years in office. As a very severe economic and social crisis hit the country during these years, the demand grew for a strong president, and in 1967 the plural executive was abolished by a referendum. In reaction to the plural executive, the 1967 constitution created a very strong presidency, took away some of the legislature's power to initiate legislation, and provided for automatic approval of bills under certain conditions when the assembly might fail to act.

The Uruguayan experience with the plural executive demonstrates how strong is the desire to limit the power of the president and yet how powerful is the desire to have a strong president. No other country in Latin American has ever tried this solution.

## Parliamentary Systems

On the other hand, parliamentary government with a cabinet responsible to the legislature has been tried several times with the hope that this would control omnipotent presidents. The most complete system of cabinet government was in Chile from 1891 to 1925; however, this never worked well because no party ever had a majority in the legislature, and so the 1925 constitution reverted to the presidential system.

A limited constitutional monarchy in Brazil from 1824 to 1889 included a parliamentary system, but the emperor was so powerful that the system was not a true parliamentary system and was dropped after the 1889 revolution, when the presidential system was instituted. In 1961, Brazil faced a constitutional crisis after an elected president suddenly resigned, leaving the presidency to a vice-president of a party representing a minority of the voters. Faced by the possibility of civil war, the legislature stripped the new president of his power by creating a parliamentary system. This new effort failed because, although the powers of the executive rested in a cabinet responsible to the Chamber of Deputies, the president had the power to appoint the prime minister. Thus, the president could, and did, appoint prime ministers who worked to destroy the parliamentary system. In one year things became so bad that the parliamentary system was abolished without ever really having had a chance to demonstrate whether it could work to limit the power of the president.

## Semi- or Quasi-Parliamentary Systems

Some writers about Latin American government refer to semi- or quasi-parliamentary systems because many constitutions have contained clauses under which cabinet ministers can attend meetings of the legislature or be questioned by the legislature, or in which the legislature can vote no-confidence in a minister or a cabinet, forcing resignation from office. Guatemala has had a constitutional clause since 1945 that provides that a minister must resign after a vote of no-confidence by the legislature. This had proved ineffective because the president can call for a revote on the confidence motion and a two-thirds vote of the total membership, which is very difficult to obtain, is required to force resignation. Even if the minister is finally voted out, the legislature has no power to force the president to appoint a new minister who will be in harmony with itself. Rather, the president has on various occasions appointed new ministers just as obnoxious as their predecessors, who followed the policies already objected to.

In Peru, during the period of constitutional government from 1963 to 1968, the legislature several times voted no-confidence in cabinet ministers who then resigned, but this never led the president to cooperate with the legislature. Eventually military dictatorship returned to Peru and there has been no legislature since then. The time span in Peru was so short that it is impossible to say whether this could have been a real check upon the executive.

In Chile the 1925 constitution did not contain a no-confidence rule, but cabinet members could be impeached by the legislature and have been from time to time. The constitutional crisis that led to the present military dictatorship came, in part, because President Allende several times broke the spirit of the constitution, if not the letter, by not removing impeached ministers. What he did was to shuffle the cabinet posts; thus, the impeached minister remained a member of the cabinet.

Similar clauses appeared in many of the constitutions adopted through the years. In all cases, however, the dominance of the presidency kept these constitutional rules from being really important limitations upon the power of the president. As long as he has had the power to appoint and remove ministers, the presidential system has remained the rule.

## Legislative Approval of Appointments

Many constitutions have included requirements that the legislature approve certain presidential appointments. This has not been a real check upon the presidents because of the general weakness of the legislatures. Another clause found in Peru, Chile, and some other countries is the rule that a president cannot leave the country without the permission of one or both houses of the legislature. Even when this power is exercised, as it was in Chile in 1969 when the Communist, Socialist, and National parties combined in the Senate to refuse to allow President Frei to visit the United States, this is not really a limit on what the president can do within the country.

## The Sharing of Executive Power

The Costa Rican constitution of 1949 made a determined effort to weaken the relative power of the president by strengthening the legislature and the judiciary, and by requiring that executive power be exercised by a president and his ministers acting together. The constitution specifies those powers to be exercised exclusively by the president, those he must exercise jointly with one of his ministers, and those to be exercised in the name of a council of government, which consists of the president and his ministers meeting formally.

Whatever the intentions of the writers of the constitution, the Costa Rican president remains a strong executive with few limits upon his actions, except for the Supreme Court's power to declare his acts unconstitutional and the legislature's power to refuse him funds. The reason for this is that, although the president needs the countersignature of a minister or the agreement of the entire cabinet, he always gets this because he appoints the cabinet ministers. Ex-President José Figueres told me that he made a deliberate attempt to strengthen the council of government by refusing at times to make his opinion known and asking the group to make a decision. He never succeeded; instead, the group would wait and refuse to make the decision until it found out his opinion. On occasion, Figueres would turn the office over to a vice-president and go to his farm to give the cabinet a chance to make decisions without him. This also failed, he reported, because a constant stream of cabinet officers kept dropping in to tell him they just happened to be driving by, and asking him what he thought about whatever their problem was. Apparently, the tradition of having the president make all important decisions is too strong to be overcome by a change in the wording of a constitution, expecially when the essential features of the presidential system are preserved and the president has the exclusive power to appoint and discharge ministers.

The same scheme is found in the present Venezuelan constitution that divides executive power so that part is exercised by the president alone, part by the president together with his council of ministers, and part by the president countersigned by a minister. As in Costa Rica, this does not limit the president, as he alone has the power to appoint and remove his ministers.

The president in many of the republics must have a cabinet minister countersign all presidential decrees and regulations, but as long as the president appoints and removes his ministers as he sees fit, this is no limitation upon his power.

## Legislative Impeachment of the President

Another attempt to limit the power of the president, copied from the U.S. Constitution, is the power of the legislative to impeach the president, thus removing him from office. Practically all constitutions have this clause. In Panama, during the campaign to elect a new president for the 1968–72 term, the legislative assembly voted to impeach President Marco A. Robles, who immediately used the national guard to prevent further meetings of the assembly. The issue went to the Supreme Court, which by a vote of 8 to 1 decided that the impeachment was illegal.

In 1950 in Colombia, the Liberal majority of the legislature decided to impeach the president for not preserving law and order during the presidential election campaign. The incumbent president, Mariano Ospina Pérez, immediately used the army to prevent the Congress from meeting. It never met again and thus could not vote the impeachment.

As these examples show, impeachment is not an easy method for removing a president from office. There have been some successful impeachments. In Panama in 1951 and 1955, respectively, Presidents Arnulfo Arias and José Ramón Guizado were impeached, but generally this method has failed to control presidents.

## Ecuador's Court of Constitutional Guarantees

Ecuador, in its 1967 constitution, tried to check the power of the president by creating a court of constitutional guarantees. This body consisted of a senator elected by the Senate, two deputies elected by the Chamber of Deputies, the president of the Supreme Court of Justice, a representative of the president of the republic, the attorney general, the president of the Supreme Electoral Tribunal, and three citizens elected by the Congress. This body was to watch for the observance of the constitution and the laws—particularly the constitutional guarantees—make suggestions about these matters, and hear complaints. When the Congress was not in session, the Court of Constitutional Guarantees could make temporary nominations for positions ordinarily filled by vote of Congress and advise the president. We do not know whether this scheme could work as a check on the president because this constitution was in force only a short time before being abrogated by a military government.

## The Creation of Independent Agencies

Another scheme devised to curtail the power of the president has been to have the constitution or the legislature create independent or semi-independent governmental agencies or institutions that are financed by public funds. Usually, each independent agency is controlled by a board of directors that the president has trouble dominating. In Costa Rica, for example, it takes about three years of a president's term before his appointees are the majority of the directing boards of the autonomous agencies. Since the Costa Rican president has a four-year term, he only really influences the activity of these groups during half of his term in office.

The independent agency has proved to be a real check upon the power of the president where constitutional government is the rule. It hampers the president in that he is not able to force the agency to follow his policy, and in some cases the president of the republic and the directors of the independent agencies have found themselves in open opposition on policy.

There seems to be no logical reason why one organization is set up as an independent agency and another is under the control of the president. In Ecuador, for example, from 1952 to 1956 independent agencies spent from 34 to 44 percent of the total national budget without any direct control by the president. At that time civil aviation, radio, telegraph, telephones, and the post office were under the minister of public works, while roads in the province of Guayas, many ports, the state railroads, and the drinking water in Manta were controlled by decentralized independent agencies.

## Other Solutions Attempted

In order to end a period of extreme political violence, Colombia, in 1958, devised a system of limiting the president's power known as the National Front. This was a method of creating a coalition government in which the presidency alternated between the country's two large parties, and all other positions—legislative, cabinet, bureaucratic, and judicial—were divided equally between the two parties. Thus, there were two very great limitations upon the power of the presidency: the difficulty of getting a majority in the legislature and the need to appoint members of the opposing party to 50 percent of the cabinet positions. While the Colombian national front system did not win universal support, it succeeded in stopping most of the violence it was created to end.

Another limitation upon the Colombian president is the council of state, composed of ten members, five from each party, elected every four years by the congress from a list of names presented by the president. The council of state must be consulted by the president in certain situations when the congress is not in session, and the advice of the council is binding in certain matters.

A few of the republics—Costa Rica, Brazil, and Colombia—have adopted judicial review of executive actions. Where the courts have been permitted to function this has been a real check upon unlimited power.

The really important check upon the president in the Latin American republics has been the power of the military, but this is no check when the military officers are themselves the executive, with a president who is a general. President Arturo Frondizi of Argentina told me he never was able to get control of the government after he was elected in 1958. Even though he appointed the first civilian minister of defense the country had ever had, and he was the constitutional commander in chief of the armed forces, he could not do what he wanted to do. After dabbling in politics for so long, the military officers believed that they had a special role to play as guardians of the constitutional order and supreme authority on the course of the nation. The officers, according to President Frondizi, were willing to let him govern, but only within the limits set by the armed forces hierarchy. When he tried to escape these limits the army arrested him, put him in jail, and appointed a more subservient president. In cases where a general is the president or where a civilian has the support of the armed forces hierarchy, his power is practically unlimited.

Most of the constitutions give the president some kind of emergency power which enables him to suspend parts of the constitution and declare a state of siege. This is something that was not taken from the U.S. Constitution, and it has been used over and over again to allow presidents to wield unlimited power.

## CONCLUSIONS

Is there anything that can be done to really limit the power of the president in Latin America? The experience of the last 150 years seems to demonstrate that power can only be checked by power. The way to limit the power of the president, therefore, is to create competing centers of power. The most important step probably would be to end the French system of local government and, through a system of universal suffrage, allow local bases of power to be created. This would strengthen political parties, and with stronger political parties more responsible presidents could be elected, and responsible oppositions created.

A second step would be to strengthen the legislatures, especially by allowing reelection where this is not allowed. All of the constitutional provisions that prevent legislatures from meeting except for limited periods should be removed from the constitutions. Salaries, staff, and offices should be provided to members of the legislatures. Given the crisis atmosphere surrounding the drive, during recent decades, for more rapid economic development, the executive has been supreme because it had almost a monopoly of technology, skills, and financial resources. Giving some of these to the legislatures would enable them to legislate more effectively and allow them to truly check the president.

The creation of an impartial bureaucracy by utilizing a system of merit appointment for the civil service would also be a check upon the activity of the president. In most of the Latin American republics this has not yet been done.

The need to build up other power centers is of the utmost importance. Political parties, trade unions, business groups, and varied interest groups, if strong and active, would be real forces for limiting the power of the president. An independent press, including radio and television, would help to create more alert public opinion. This is recognized by all of the executives whose power we are talking about limiting. That is why the military dictators and the overpowerful presidents refuse to allow a free press and prevent the growth of strong political parties, trade unions, and interest groups.

Eternal vigilance remains the price of liberty, and it is almost impossible to preserve liberty and limit the power of the executive when the press is shackled, trade unions and political parties are harrassed and prevented from functioning, and opposition to the president is looked upon as treason. Until such independent centers of power are created, the omnipotent executive will remain the center of political power in Latin America.

## BIBLIOGRAPHICAL NOTES

Very little has been written about limitations on the powers of the president in the Latin American republics. The constitutional provisions and the legal checks and balances can be reviewed in Amos J. Peaslee, *Constitutions of Nations,* rev. 3rd ed., vol. 4 (The Hague: Martinus Nijhoff, 1970). On the executive in general and how the presidential system functions, see Harold E. Davis, "The Presidency," in his *Government and Politics in Latin America* (New York: Ronald Press, 1958), pp. 252–89; Alexander T. Edelman, "Executives: Democratic Caesars and Democrats," in his *Latin American Government and Politics* (Homewood, Ill.: Dorsey Press, 1969), pp. 406–42; Russell H. Fitzgibbon, "Executive Power in Central America," *Journal of Politics* 3 (August 1941): 297–307; Rosendo A. Gomez, "Latin American Executives: Essence and Variation," *Journal of Inter-American Studies* 3 (January 1961): 81–95; Miguel Jorrin, "The Executive Power," in his *Governments of Latin America* (New York: Van Nostrand, 1953), pp. 77–79; Karl Loewenstein, "The Presidency Outside the United States," *Journal of Politics* 11 (August 1949): 447–96; William W. Pierson and Federico G. Gil, "The Executive," in their *Governments of Latin America* (New York: McGraw-Hill, 1957), pp. 208–41; William S. Stokes, "Omnipotent Executive Power," in his *Latin*

*American Politics* (New York: Thomas Y. Crowell, 1959), pp. 385–411; Frank Tannenbaum, "Personal Government in Mexico," *Foreign Affairs* 27 (October 1948): 44–57; and Arpad von Lazar, "Latin American Executives and their Roles," in his *Latin American Politics: A Primer* (Boston: Allyn and Bacon, 1971), pp. 30–35.

On denying reelection to presidents, see Harold E. Davis, "The Principle of Nonreelection," in op. cit., pp. 268–71.

On Uruguay's plural executive system, see Alexander T. Edelman, "The Rise and Demise of Uruguay's Second Plural Executive," *Journal of Politics* 41 (February 1969): 119–39; Russell H. Fitzgibbon, "Adoption of a Collegiate Executive in Uruguay," *Journal of Politics* 14 (November 1952): 616–42; William W. Pierson and Federico G. Gil, "The Uruguayan Experiments," in op. cit., pp. 212–15; and Milton I. Vanger, "Uruguay Introduces Government by Committee," *American Political Science Review* 48 (June 1954): 500–13.

On parliamentary government in Latin America, see William S. Stokes, "Parliamentary Government in Latin America," *American Political Science Review* 39 (June 1945): 522–36.

On limiting presidential power by splitting executive power between a president and his cabinet, see Harry Kantor, "The Executive in Costa Rica," in his *Patterns of Politics and Political Systems in Latin America* (Chicago: Rand McNally, 1969), pp. 216–17, and Leo B. Lott, "The Executive Branch of Government in Venezuela," in his *Venezuela and Paraguay: Political Modernity and Tradition in Conflict* (New York: Holt, Rinehart, and Winston, 1971), pp. 283–97.

On judicial review see J. A. C. Grant, "Judicial Control of the Constitutionality of Statutes and Administrative Legislation in Colombia: Nature and Evolution of the Present System," *Southern California Law Review* 23 (July 1950): 484–504.

# 3

## MEXICO'S AUTHORITARIAN
## PRESIDENCY
### Kenneth F. Johnson

## THE MEXICAN PRESIDENCY: A CONTEMPORARY OVERVIEW

Out of the Mexican Revolution of 1910–17 emerged a new style of Mexican political life. It became known as single-party democracy presided over by an authoritarian president. Both the constitution of 1917 and established precedence have since endowed the Mexican president with strong governing prerogatives. Among other things the president has the power to intervene in state and local governments and to replace their elected magistrates by decree. He has strong powers of the purse over all levels of government, and although the national legislature has a paper veto this power has not been exercised over an executive since the late 1920s. The president may expel foreigners and their companies. He is invested with extensive powers to protect the internal security of the nation. "Security" can have various meanings, including security from verbal assault; that is, the president has de facto power of press and media censorship. In recent years such censorship has become a hallmark of the Mexican presidency, further underscoring its authoritarian bent. Also, the president is given the power to carry out land distribution and to promote collective bargaining rights for workers. In the past the degree of use of such powers has depended upon the nature of the incumbent, and upon the socio-economic-political milieu in which he found himself. The president is, finally, to be a guarantor of all constitutional freedoms; he can also take them away. In short, the Mexican president can be authoritarian.

The single-party governing institution which Mexico has evolved is known as the PRI (Institutional Revolutionary party). It is the president's key power instrument and he sits at its apex, like the ancient sacrificial priest or *tlatoani* of the Aztecs who meted out justice and well-being, but whose dicta were not to be questioned.[1] The official party is superimposed over the government and the two are made to appear as if they were one organic whole. Groups outside the PRI's vast penumbra are not allowed real participation. And there are many such groups, satellite parties and associations that increase (along with Mexico's burgeoning 3.5 percent annual birth rate) all too rapidly for the single-party system to absorb them. Thus, political alienation is spawned. It runs the gamut from abstentionism during elections to guerrilla insurgency, and constitutes one of the problems that increasingly occupies the attention of contemporary Mexican presidents. A concomitant dilemma is how to control public expressions of political alienation in a single-party system that propagates the mystique of one, unchallengable, official truth.

Probably no president during the twentieth century controlled political alienation so well as did Lázaro Cárdenas (1934–40), but then he had a quite favorable environment in which to work. His land distribution and subsoil expropriation programs attracted a wide popular following. Cárdenas was said to have spent more time out with the people than in his office. He is remembered today as a prototype for the "benevolent authoritarian" that the Mexican president tries to be. Cárdenas was independent. He refused to be a puppet for his predecessor Plutarco Elías Calles and even had the latter expelled from Mexico. Since then, presidents have tried to establish themselves as unique entities, as creative revolutionaries, with a giant "R." Each has sought to leave his own legacy for history to record, but without outwardly repudiating that of his predecessor as Cárdenas did. This became critical as alienation against the single-party monolith intensified during the 1970s and as that alienation, in turn, was rewarded with government repression.

An oft-quoted dictum of Frank Brandenburg holds that Mexicans "avoid personal dictatorship by retiring their dictators every six years."[2] This was a part of the denouement of the revolution: no immediate reelection of the president and, in effect, no reelection at all. One president, Alvaro Obregón, who sought to violate this dictum, was assassinated in 1928. Presidents since Cárdenas have sought to perpetuate their influence through a unique process for choosing successors. And each president has tried to select a compatible successor, just as did Cárdenas. His successor, Manuel Avila Camacho (1940–46), guided Mexico through World War II. Avila also engineered significant consolidations within the single-party system, leaving the PRI with its contemporary name and its present subdivision into three basic sectors: agrarian, labor, and popular. Next, Miguel Alemán (1946–52) used a hard hand in stimulating postwar economic development, especially in collaboration with U.S. interests. In this way he undid some of the hard feelings left by the oil expropriations of the Cárdenas era. Alemán's successor, Adolfo Ruiz Cortines (1952–58), made notable efforts to professionalize the federal bureaucracy and to instill honesty into Mexican politics. He seems to have been the last Mexican president to have attempted a serious rationalization of the governing system.

By the time of the presidency of Adolfo López Mateos (1958–64), Mexico was changing from a predominantly rural to an urban nation. Population pressures were increasing on the cities. Rural discontent grew. The inability of the PRI to be all things to all people was showing itself. López Mateos inherited labor unrest: the workers of the government-owned and operated railroads led by Demetrio Vallejo and Valentín Campa, attempted to paralyze transportation in the spring of 1959. They were put down forcefully by the army under the president's direction. The leaders of that strike received harsh prison terms of 16 years each.[3] At this point, the image of a "benevolent" president was weakened, while the "authoritarian" part of the equation was reinforced.

A crucial point in the further atrophy of the presidential mystique came during the regime of Gustavo Díaz Ordaz (1964–70). It was his fate to play sacrificial priest to several hundred students who died in a government-ordered massacre at Tlatelolco, near downtown Mexico City, on the night of October 2, 1968. Thousands were injured and the true death toll may never be known. Tlatelolco became a symbol of the division between the people and the regime, between the official party and the congeries of satellite parties and "out groups." It was Díaz Ordaz' own cabinet minister, Luis Echeverría (minister of *Gobernación*), who shared much of the public opprobrium over the Tlatelolco disaster; the same Echeverría succeeded to the presidency for the *sexenio* that ended in 1976.[4]

## ECHEVERRÍA: THE PRESIDENT AS POLITICAL ACTOR

To be sure, the authoritarian governing tradition was carried on by Luis Echeverría, but he added his own personal style to it, as the distinguished Mexican scholar Daniel Cosío Villegas has noted.[5] There was perhaps more publicly reported violence in Mexico during the Echeverría regime than ever before. Guerrillas led by Genaro Vásquez Rojas organized in the hills of Guerrero and began a series of spectacular kidnappings of elitists and attacks on military and police garrisons. When Vásquez died in 1972 his cause was taken up by Lucio Cabañas, who proclaimed a "party of the poor." The kidnappings and assassinations continued. By the time of Cabañas' death in 1974 a plethora of violent groups had formed. President Echeverría was their ultimate goal, but many wealthy oligarchs were kidnapped or assassinated as surrogate targets. While the ultraleft reminded the poor that Echeverría was the assassin of Tlatelolco, the rich accused the president of being soft on the extremists and of contributing to an atmosphere in which terrorism could flourish. Eventually, the terror was visited upon the international diplomatic community; rightly or wrongly, much of this was blamed on Echeverría. His response was to mobilize troops for war against the guerrillas.

The new president had inaugurated his regime with increased student repression. On June 10, 1971, in the San Cosme neighborhood of Mexico City, a student march was disrupted by government-supported terrorists called the "Falcons" (*los Halcones*), who were transported in government buses and given police protection. A number of students were killed, many more wounded, and even the national press corps was attacked. The scandal was so open that President Echeverría had to ask for the resignation of several high-ranking officials (including two cabinet ministers) in order to maintain his innocence. The bulk of the testimony and evidence indicates that Echeverría knew about the Falcons and approved of them even though he insisted otherwise.[6] The victimized students at San Cosme were protesting, among other things, the continued incarceration of student leaders from Tlatelolco. Echeverría promised the public a full investigation of the San Cosme repression, but when his sexenio ended some six years later no such report had appeared. Presidential secrecy was the prevailing mode. The people, in the end, could not be trusted with their own constitutional right to know. To the Echeverría regime, maintenance of the official image of the state, especially vis-a-vis the outside world, was more important than guaranteeing a free press or the freedom to protest, via peaceful means, what were perceived as abuses of power.

All of this becomes curious when one considers that much of the Echeverría period was devoted to molding an image of Mexico as a leader among the Third World countries. Echeverría himself openly sought the secretary-generalship of the United Nations as his term came to a close in 1976. Since that post is hardly one for which a public campaign has traditionally been mounted, it seems that Luis Echeverría had a personal need for deference and status, as well as accumulation of political power. This is a key point, because the Mexican presidency allows its incumbent to make almost anything he wants of it. Constitutional provisions are mere formalisms that have been amplified by precedent. The president has practically limitless power. If he should so choose, the president can be a great internal reformer like Cárdenas, or he can become an international image builder like Echeverría.

Luis Echeverría exemplified the degree to which the authoritarianism inherent in his office could be used to fit the personal style of the incumbent, in this case the style of an insatiable power seeker. Since he wanted to impress the world, and especially the developing nations, with his statemanship it will be instructive to examine selected external views of the Echeverría presidency as it came to an end in 1976.

At one extreme in the Western Hemisphere, an editorial in the generally conservative *La Prensa* of Buenos Aires (May 12, 1976) revealed preoccupation in both Argentina and the United States with the leftist direction in which President Echeverría was steering Mexico. Feelings were reported, from both those countries, that Echeverría's regime had "modalities" comparable to those of the Marxist regime of the late Salvador Allende in Chile, as well as to those of Fidel Castro. Commenting on the president's drive for Third World leadership, *La Prensa* said, "no other Mexican president spent so much time outside his country—ten large journeys in five years extending from the African jungles to Russia and to the deserts of the Middle East." The editorial also noted that while Echeverría preached openness and friendship toward the outside world his government voted in the United Nations to condemn Israel. In addition, *La Prensa* charged that, while Mexican embassies about the world were places of refuge for political refugees, terrorists, and hijackers, at home in Mexico criticism of the regime was castigated with utmost severity. This is evidence that Echeverría's tough hand in domestic politics had not escaped the attention of other nations, especially vis-a-vis Echeverría's preferred image abroad. *La Prensa* even reminded the Third World of the Tlatelolco massacre as an example of the Echeverría governmental style.

The Western Hemisphere paid a great deal of attention to the Echeverría regime's attitude toward the military dictatorship that emerged in Chile following the overthrow of its constitutional government in 1973. Echeverría sent a personal airplane to bring back Dr. Allende's widow and family. The Mexican embassy accepted dozens of political exiles, and ultimately many more were sent to Mexico in response to Echeverría's criticisms of the Chilean junta before the United Nations and the Organization of American States (OAS). Mexico severed diplomatic relations with Chile in 1974 as a further gesture of protest against what Echeverría ostentatiously challenged as violations of human rights by the Pinochet regime. In 1976 Echeverría announced that his government would boycott a meeting of OAS ministers in Santiago, saying that participating would be tantamount to recognizing Pinochet. Later that year he seized upon the Chilean theme once more. He denounced unspecified "emissaries of the past" in Mexico who were allegedly planning a military coup against him, and cited the recent military interventions in Argentina and Chile as cases in point. According to *Excelsior,* at that time the most influential Mexican daily, Echeverría declared publicly that "there will never be a Pinochet in Mexico."[7] The president then condemned a secret meeting that was to have taken place in the northern industrial city of Monterrey, usually a center of opposition to the regime in Mexico City, for financing a "fascist style" resistance to his regime.[8] He also referred to a "small plutocratic and profascist minority which sought to alter the growing rhythm of the Mexican Revolution."[9]

It is a revealing irony of Echeverría's style that as his presidency drew to a close he was consistently preoccupied with authoritarian conspiracies against him and with authoritarianism (fascism) of one sort or another around the world; meanwhile, he was reacting in the most authoritarian way to critics of his own regime at home. This leads to consideration of one of the most fateful decisions of Echeverría's career, one that left him open to the most severe charge of authoritarianism, indeed of totalitarianism. Echeverría decided to close the newspaper *Excelsior* during July 1976. This publication was a bastion of intellectual and press freedom in Mexico. *Excelsior* was a cooperative in which the workers owned shares. Its editors were dedicated to open, critical journalism. And *Excelsior* was one of the best newspapers printed in the Spanish language. Echeverría's act was nearly equivalent to President Nixon's having taken over the Washington *Post* at the height of the Watergate controversy.

During most of the Echeverría sexenio *Excelsior* was filled with stories of popular uprisings against corrupt government officials around the country, plus penetrating investigative reporting on a number of sensitive themes, including intra-PRI power struggles, corruption in general, and poverty. It was difficult for Echeverría to continue to promote himself as a leader of the Third World who merited the secretary-generalship of the United Nations, when critical observers pointed out that he presided over a country with some 40 percent of its work force unemployed and over 70 percent of that work force earning less than 80 dollars per month, a nation in the humiliating position of "solving" its surplus labor problem by encouraging millions to undertake illegal migration to the United States (and then accusing North America of "racism" for expelling the "wetbacks").[10]

Echeverría's paranoid style was anathema to the image he sought to project to the outside world: he proclaimed Mexico as the land of "*apertura democrática*" (democratic openness) and of "*autocrítica*" (a form of self-criticism). He denounced U.S. racism and great power hegemony over the Third World economies. He condemned Israel for its Zionist "imperialism." He paid tribute to the populism of Juan Perón and self-righteously condemned the Argentine generals who overthrew the Peronist regime when it degenerated into government by sheer terror, after having produced the world's worst rate of inflation in 1976.[11] Echeverría condemned a group of Mexican student critics in March 1975 as fascists working for the CIA (the president himself had previously collaborated with the CIA, as cited below). Then he closed *Excelsior* and replaced it with a puppet newspaper published irreverently under the same name.

Echeverría came to power using the slogan "*arriba y adelante,*" "up and forward." But such movement did not occur in Mexico in any meaningful sense. As Echeverría's six-year term drew to a close, the image he left behind throughout much of the hemisphere is perhaps best reflected by this editorial from the New York *Times* on the closing of *Excelsior,* a reflection of just how much up and forward Mexico had come under Echeverría's style of presidential action.

> Almost immediately after the presidential election [of 1976], a well-financed rebellion was organized [by the government] within the paper's staff to create

a situation in which the editors risked armed conflict if they sought to carry out their normal duties. The editors bowed to the threat of force and quit their employment. The bully boys of Lenin in 1917 or of Hitler in 1933 could not have done a more efficient job of enslaving a once proud and free newspaper. But this act of totalitarian suppression discredits those who now boast of Mexico's stability and democracy.[12]

In point of fact, Echeverría had not fooled much of the Third World, especially not Latin America. An article in the influential daily *La Opinión,* of Buenos Aires, referred to the Mexican elections of 1976 as part of the ongoing "six-year ritual" and noted the use by the PRI of coercion in bringing peasants to political rallies to create the facade of enthusiasm for the regime.[13] Everyone knew that only one candidate to succeed Echeverría was on the ballot, and that public money was being spent to finance an empty ritual. An appropriate question was raised: "To what extent is democracy possible and popular participation meaningful within a political structure which offers no visible alternatives?"[14]

## ROOTS AND MACHINATIONS OF POWER: THE MAKING OF PRESIDENTS

### The "Unveiling" Procedure

In his book, *La sucesión presidencial,* published in 1975, Daniel Cosío Villegas cites the controversial testimony of ex-CIA agent Philip Agee to the effect that Luis Echeverría knew he had been picked to succeed President Díaz Ordaz as early as 1966, that is, four years before the formal nominating procedure would take place.[15] Agee wrote that Echeverría, then minister of Gobernación, had confided this to the CIA station head in Mexico City. Gobernación is a political power center in Mexico and it is a frequent source of presidential candidates. Much of this power comes from the access to intelligence information that the minister of Gobernación enjoys. Gobernación is roughly a mix of the U.S. justice and interior departments.

The Agee testimony supports the widespread belief that the CIA and other U.S. intelligence agencies collaborate closely with Gobernación and its subsidiary, the Mexican Federal Judicial Police. Agee identified both Echeverría and Díaz Ordaz as former CIA collaborators. It is noteworthy that Cosío Villegas cited Agee as an authoritative source. Cosío Villegas, one of Mexico's most respected political historians, is distinguished for his works on the Mexican presidency and the political system generally. He has known most recent presidents personally, especially Luis Echeverría.[16]

Significantly, Cosío made reference to the Agee book in the context of demonstrating part of his own thesis about the Mexican presidential succession, that is, that the president makes his selection fairly early during his term and hides it as best he can until he is forced by pressures from within the PRI to declare himself.[17] Were he to announce his successor before the final year of his term, the incumbent president might progressively lose power and thereby impair his ability to carry out programs intended to carve him a distinct place in Mexico's political history. The president has, however, an intriguing procedure for testing his power structure's reaction to a potential successor. There is a political folklore in Mexico about "veiled ones" called "*tapados*" who are suspected to be the president's choice of successor. But there is only one real, or "*verdadero,*" tapado, and he is formally "unveiled" at the official party's national nominating convention.

In point of fact, however, the unveiling may occur in other and quite informal ways. For instance, the name of a given tapado may be leaked to the government-controlled press while the president and his advisors await a reaction from within the PRI. There were also external reactions to be considered, for example, that of the United States. Because of the close interdependency of the Mexican and North American economies, the Mexican presidential succession is a matter of importance north of the Rio Grande. The CIA, as special "policeman" protecting U.S. interests abroad (as Agee put it), will also be interested in the new Mexican president. Thus, if Echeverría did declare himself to the CIA station chief, this was undoubtedly a "trial balloon" of sorts. It was especially significant in the light of the then forthcoming Olympic Games, considering the CIA's interest in them (as per Agee's testimony) and in view of the fact that Echeverría would be the minister principally charged with defending that international event against any threat of attack (and student protests had already been voiced in 1966). How the U.S. power structure felt about Echeverría was clearly important to the presidential decision of 1970—apparently the American feedback was favorable.

Early in *La sucesión presidencial,* Cosío treats the works of several North American scholars who found the selection of PRI candidates to follow certain logical rules explained by pendulum theories or by schemes of requisites of a personal and professional nature, in which the final selection is of someone capable of balancing opposing forces. Cosío finds it interesting that the North Americans see the Mexican process so rationally and clearly, while the Mexican "insiders" themselves do not see it that way at all. He specifically questions what he sees as a general North American unwillingness to admit that the Mexican presidential succession is resolved "arbitrarily and capriciously" that leads those analysts into the error of creating elaborate schemes of kingmakers and power theories to explain the selection process.[18]

There is more to the Cosío thesis. He argues carefully that the legendary Lázaro Cárdenas saw to it that his successor was a man like Avila Camacho, one who would rectify the shortcomings in the outgoing president's legacy, but who would do so slowly and quietly so that the rectification would not imply "condemnation," and Cárdenas' image in history would be preserved as truly revolutionary.[19] Cosío Villegas is one of the best-informed scholars of the Mexican presidency and his opinions are to be taken seriously. He is saying, in effect, that the outgoing president follows a tradition set by Cárdenas of controlling the selection process so as to guarantee that he will not be repudiated by his successor. In addition, he must choose a successor who will allow the outgoing president to retain residual powers even as the former attends realistically to the glaring needs of the nation. He must make the choice early and then test it informally via the ritual of the tapados.

During 1976 a Mexican journalist from the capital city confirmed to me much of the Cosío Villegas thesis and threw additional light on the antecedents of that year's presidential succession. The story (and I have agreed to respect the confidence of the source) is one that can easily be verified or rejected by almost any biographical scholar of the outgoing president, Luis Echeverría. Throughout Mexico great surprise was felt when it was learned that José López Portillo (the treasury secretary), not Mario Moya Palencia (of Gobernación), would be the next president.[20] Most observers had believed that Moya was to be the next president. It seems, however, that Echeverría and López Portillo were close college companions who, sometime in the 1940s or early 1950s, took an ocean cruise to Chile for study purposes. Furthermore, it is alleged that the only nonfamily person invited to Echeverría's wedding was José López Portillo. Moreover, it is said that a very intimate personal relationship existed between the two during the Echeverría sexenio, and that López Portillo was Echeverría's principal behind-the-scenes advisor and secret choice of successor all along, even while an attempt was made to give the impression that Moya Palencia was the chief "mover" in the cabinet.

It is natural that observers expect the secretary of Gobernación to succeed to the presidency, as occurred in 1964 and 1970. Moya was a major power figure. His ministry has great ascriptive powers. Gobernación, after all, has control over the Mexican equivalents of the U.S. FBI and CIA (although nearly every Mexican governmental department has its own secret police of one ilk or another). Gobernación has the most complete and effective intelligence operation in the Mexican republic; hence, the head of that department is de facto one of Mexico's most feared men, much as J. Edgar Hoover was feared in the United States. It is Gobernación that has the files on "everyone." If it is necessary to leak something unfavorable to the government-controlled press that will diminish a certain power contender within or outside the official PRI, it is almost surely Gobernación that will be called upon to do the leaking. As cited above, Presidents Luis Echeverría and Díaz Ordaz were both former secretaries of Gobernación.

What is significant is the fact that all Mexican knowledgeables I interviewed in the months following the unveiling, or *destape,* on September 22, 1975 considered the matter a mystery. Moreover, Cosío Villegas produced a

book following the destape in which he admits that the matter was then a
mystery to him, too.[21] My Mexican informants told me that "when Cosío
Villegas does not know, or is not saying, that in itself is significant." This tends
to confirm, of course, Cosío's contention that the selection may very well be
made arbitrarily and capriciously.

In his latest and last book, *La sucesión: desenlace y perspectivas,* Cosío
related the surprising story of how the unveiling of López Portillo occurred.
(Cosío prefers to call the 1975 unveiling *"el corcholatazo,"* or the "uncorking,"
which conveys better the element of mystery and surprise.) It was done quite
informally and under almost bizarre circumstances. He says that late in the
afternoon of September 22, Moya Palencia and some colleagues were lunching
in an unidentified place, but to which reporters apparently had access. Their
meal was interrupted by newspapermen carrying copies of *Ultimas Noticias de
Excelsior* announcing the unveiling of López Portillo. Apparently, they were
all surprised that the news was out but confirmed it while Moya Palencia tried
to maintain his composure. Cosío relates further the rumor, which he then
discredits, that the president in fact had arranged to have the announcement
emerge as a surprise and that he, Echeverría, had selected the weakest of the
potential tapados, in order to keep him indebted after the transfer of power
in 1976. Note that, while Cosío discredits this rumor, he nevertheless repeats
it.[22]

It was believed that almost all the state governors and key leaders of the
PRI's sectoral organizations (labor, agrarian, and popular sectors) had endorsed Moya Palencia's informal candidacy to become the verdadero tapado.
So Echeverría clearly dumped Moya. It is rumored that a power struggle had
developed between Moya and Echeverría, and that this fight became open
during 1975. The most patent aspects of the struggle concerned governorships.
In April of 1975 Echeverría's handpicked governor of the state of Hidalgo,
Otoniel Miranda, was deposed by the state legislature after only 29 days in
office.[23] My informants claim that the fall of the Hidalgo governor was the
indirect work of Moya Palencia, who perhaps feared that someone other than
himself could become the verdadero tapado and who therefore sought a confrontation with President Echeverría to force the issue publicly. This did not
happen, and the gubernatorial arena yielded later on a more clearly defined
confrontation in Sonora during October 1975. There, under orders from
Echeverría and with the helpless acquiescence of Moya Palencia (who by then
had been passed over for the presidency), Governor Carlos Armando Biebrich
was deposed by the state legislature and replaced with Sonora's incumbent
senator, Alejandro Carrillo Marcor. It was the first time since 1935 that
Mexico City had so intervened in Sonora's state government.[24]

Space does not permit telling the entire saga of Governor Biebrich's
downfall, but he was involved in several international scandals including arms
and narcotics. In addition, in the fall of 1975, Biebrich ordered the assassina-

tion of a number of peasant squatters and pretended he had approval from President Echeverría and Moya Palencia—which he did not.[25] Biebrich had been a protege of Moya, and it was rumored that should Moya become president Biebrich would be elevated to the cabinet post of Gobernación, just a step away from the presidency. The scandals, and Moya's continuing efforts to protect Biebrich, may have figured prominently in Echeverría's decision to drop Moya, if in fact he had ever been considered. There is evidence in the extradition indictments eventually brought against Biebrich that his abuse of public office had been going on for most of the three years that he had been Sonora's governor.[26] It is not likely that Moya was unaware of this, given the number of public protests against Biebrich emanating from Sonora. If these considerations entered into President Echeverría's decision not to choose Moya, one may surmise that the president had acted in the best interest of Mexico.

## The Formal Presidential Image

In considering the roots of presidential power in Mexico, one must be aware of the tradition of not personally attacking the president while he is in office. Obviously, the "out groups" and satellite parties are not bound by all the PRI may consider to be traditional, but until 1968 there had been a national taboo against venomous personal attacks on the chief executive. That was abandoned in 1968 when the protesting students demanded the death of President Díaz Ordaz and his minister Luis Echeverría. Later, when Echeverría as president was denounced in 1971 and assaulted in 1975, it became patent that both the man and the institution of the presidency had fallen into disrepute vis-a-vis the young intelligentsia. Loss of face before this sector must have wounded a determined power seeker like Echeverría badly, and some of his extreme reactions to criticism as his term came to a close (like taking over *Excelsior*) may have stemmed from the cumulative psychological impact of his clashes with students in, for example, 1968, 1971, and 1975.

The president's sensitivity to criticism, and vulnerability to attack, came to light during March 1975. Echeverría had accepted an invitation to speak at the opening of classes at the National University (UNAM) on March 14 in order to enter into a dialogue with students. The meeting was to be held in the medical faculty's auditorium named after the late Salvador Allende of Chile. The rector, Guillermo Soberón, tried to introduce the president. He was interrupted with insults and charges that "LEA (acronym for the president's name) is a fascist." The president wanted to speak. There were more insults. The student body president tried to speak and said something about the need in Mexico for a congressional investigation of CIA activities as recently disclosed by the Philip Agee book. He was shouted down as a traitor and more verbal disparagement was hurled at the president of the republic. Then the violence became physical, with gunfire; bottles and rocks were thrown. One of these wounded Echeverría in the forehead. Shortly before this, the president had shouted that the insurgent students were "pro-fascists, manipulated by the CIA, who emulate the youth corps of Hitler and Mussolini."[27] The student leader Joel Ortega replied that it was Echeverría who was propagating fascism by sending police agents into the university and by allowing labor bosses to impede development of a free labor movement in Mexico.[28]

What is significant in this is that, despite the merits of the various charges hurled back and forth, the president had been forced to retreat from dialogue with the students, and this was covered in the national press. The fact that *Excelsior* criticized the student behavior editorially did not compensate for its having printed their words and points of view. *Excelsior* also opened its pages to paid notices by radical student groups that denounced Echeverría and the PRI. Undoubtedly, this contributed to the president's determination to close that publication the following year.

We may say, then, that one of the key roots of the power of the Mexican presidency is its formal image. It does not matter that everyone knows the president sends police agents to harass students, maintains paramilitary squads to beat up them and the press corps, and presides over a regime in which corrupt labor bosses enslave the workers in conspiracy with management. What does matter is the formal image that the public communications media can forge. Perhaps the classic statement of this principle came from one-time PRI President Carlos Madrazo, who was deposed by President Díaz Ordaz in 1965 over the former's proposal to democratize the PRI via a scheme of local primaries to nominate candidates. Just as the fateful holocaust of Tlatelolco in 1968 was building up, Madrazo told a capital city reporter, "Do you know what one of Díaz Ordaz' ministers told me the other day? He said the people didn't count. What does count is the impression we create with our newspapers."[29] In other words, it may be that the "emperor has no clothes"—just don't print it publicly.


## CONCLUSIONS: LESSONS OF THE PAST, AND POTENTIAL FUTURES


### The PRI and the Presidential Succession

In a book published just prior to the presidential succession of 1970, José C. Valadés set forth some suggestive propositions relating to the presidency that can be compared with the later conclusions of Cosío Villegas. Valadés

argues that during the decade of the 1930s the Mexican population was sub-
missive enough to the political system to permit presidents to designate their
successors with little risk. But 30 years later, with Mexico's demographic
explosion, the population would not fit under the PRI's umbrella, nor even
under its penumbra.[30] There were vast youth interests, crystallized at Tlatelolco, that were effectively divorced from the official political system. This
would be a continuing threat to the PRI and to its presidents, as would be the
acute and growing pauperism in urban slums and among rural peasants. Yet,
the corrupt private interests underlying the power of high functionaries who
surrounded the president made it difficult for him to be a true reformist and
respond to critical needs. Indeed, it may not have been in the president's
personal interest to be a reformer, for the corruption had spread beyond the
limits of officialdom and was part of the society itself.[31]

Valadés says that Mexico's presidents have an inherent need to keep the
people humiliated while pretending to do otherwise, but that a statesman with
heroic valor, prudence, reformist spirit, and true modesty could return the
presidential selection process to the people and restore democracy. This would
change the authoritarian character of the Mexican presidency, but of course
it is more easily proposed than achieved.[32]

Two critical facts must be understood about the PRI and the presidency,
according to Valadés. One is that the PRI is a political bureau at the service
of the president: that is its primary task. The second is that the PRI is not really
a party because, except in its early years, it has lacked a program of definable
policies. For this reason, the PRI cannot allow genuine competition from a real
political party with a clearly defined program. The PRI is a vast elite class,
surrounding an authoritarian president, but the class holds many dissimilar,
and often contradictory, elements.[33] The class may also appear as a kind of
army without arms, but that employs various mafias—the army, secret police,
paramilitary squads, and so on—to control others and protect itself. Thus, the
undemocratic practice of selecting presidents by *dedazo* and *tapadismo* (personal designation via a secret process of tapados) is perpetuated to keep the
president's authority immune from public accountability, and from public
dialogue, except at his convenience. Thus, the president is responsible only to
a handful of kingmakers and *camarillas* (political cliques) who help him ignore
the needs of society while pretending to do otherwise.[34]

What Mexico needed from the succession of 1970, said Valadés, was a
leader who met two criteria: that he not be picked by the outgoing president,
but by a national convention, and that he not be indebted to the outgoing
president, but be forced to win popular support on his own merits.[35] Again,
this was more easily proposed than achieved, given PRI tradition. But Valadés
saw the nation as exhausted with presidential successions and the continued
use of the PRI as a personal power bureau for the president. The public disgust
was visible in popular discredit of the electoral process as a sham, a widespread

disheartened feeling vis-a-vis politics, disdain of deputies and senators, and the general helplessness and uselessness of the national congress.[36] Where, he asked, is the legislation that regulates those who make life wretched for the masses, both rural and urban? The revitalization of the congress is imperative if Mexican presidents are going to return to the people those prerogatives that were originally theirs. The congress is now a rubber stamp, a part of the president's political bureau.[37] As Valadés wrote: "It is no exaggeration to say that in only a very few countries do presidents have at their grasp the power which Mexico's president personally enjoys."[38]

Valadés points to the personal designation, or dedazo, as one of the chief evils in the system that can and must eventually lead to designation of a president who will damage the nation severely. As he analyzed the presidential succession of 1970, he saw the people asking, "Why even vote if only the official candidate can win?" This question came to preoccupy high officials of the PRI in 1975 and 1976 as the legitimacy of the regime was being called into question by voter abstentionism and the other forms of repudiation previously cited. Ultimately, the PRI was the only party on the ballot in 1976.[39]

Finally, Valadés explains that it is not the PRI that is invincible (since the PRI lacks popular grass roots, what he calls engranaje propio), but rather it is the president who is invincible because he controls the PRI. This will continue as long as the president is selected by a handful of men or by his predecessor alone; that is, the PRI will never become a true party until it is democratized.

This, then, was a direct plea to the Mexican president-to-be of 1970 to democratize the party system. Published in 1969, the work does not refer to Luis Echeverría by name. But the image depicted is clearly one of a dominant class, calling itself a party, that is really the government in disguise, and of a decidedly authoritarian president who could reform things if he wanted to. In addition, Valadés saw popular resistance efforts, however justified they might be, as doomed to the failure of anarchy—anarchy that could not triumph over the dominant class that was the PRI of 1970.

## The Nature of Authoritarian Presidency

Let us now skip to the 1976 presidential succession in Mexico. Here are some propositions in the light of Daniel Cosío Villegas' key work on the Echeverría presidency, El estilo personal de gobernar, as related to other works and evidence.

Is it the Mexican presidency per se, or is it the entire regime, that is inherently authoritarian? Valadés seems to say that the presidency is inherently authoritarian and this, in turn, makes the regime conform to its image. In this regard, the American scholar Evelyn P. Stevens' investigation argued that Mexico's political system was not oriented toward the "formulation and modification of goals through pluralistic participation in the decision-making process. Instead, we see repression of authentic interest groups and encouragement of spurious groups that can be relied on not to speak out of turn. The regime deals with bona fide groups almost as if they were enemy nations."[40] The question then is, does this characteristic behavior originate in the regime or in the presidency? Valadés says the presidency, Cosío Villegas seems to be saying the regime, and this writer's personal experience tends to affirm Cosío. Yet there is no doubt about the president's practically limitless power.

What has been the recent thrust of the Mexican presidency vis-a-vis the state's capability for generating and distributing wealth? According to Cosío's analysis, President Cárdenas sought to push the entire nation toward a more equitable distribution of existing wealth. But since the presidency of Miguel Alemán (1946–52), emphasis has been on creating centers of abundant wealth and hoping that some of this wealth would rub off on the population. The result, of course, has been the underlying motive of the student rebellion of 1968—a situation in which a privileged 10 percent of the families control 50 percent of the national income.[41] Valadés shares the spirit of this judgment.[42]

What impact has the Mexican presidency had on the myth or reality of governmental federalism? Like his successors, Echeverría extended federal control at the expense of local initiative and autonomy. He even allowed the Sonora legislature to modify the state constitution in 24 hours, thereby reducing the governor's required age to 30 to allow the election of Biebrich, who was imposed from Mexico City with the president's acquiescence.[43] This, as we have seen, Echeverría was later to regret because of the implications the Biebrich scandals had for the presidential succession. It further dramatizes what is perhaps the Achilles' heel of the Mexican system, that is, the flaunting of federal prerogatives at the expense of local autonomy where the critical problems await solution. Evidence during recent years shows a high incidence of popular, anomic, and violent uprisings and protests against corrupt local governments (especially as reported by *Excelsior* during 1975–76).

Can major errors in long-range policy conduct be attributed directly to Echeverría? To give one example, Cosío Villegas argues that Echeverría was at fault in urging agrarian reform as a way to greater industrial prosperity, rather than having championed the betterment of the rural *ejidatarios* (peasants who are members and part owners of a collective farm) as an end in itself.[44] He blames Echeverría for acquiescing in a scheme to dispossess hundreds of ejidatarios in Nayarit to permit building of a vacation center for military personnel and a facility for tourists.[45] Here, "development" was sought at the expense of those who needed it most.

Is the authoritarianism of the Mexican president to be explained in terms of historical thrust and personal psychic qualities? Translating from Cosío's conclusion, the demand by presidents like Díaz Ordaz and Echeverría for popular veneration owes much to psychic and historical factors, to be sure, but "it is due also to our political system, whose principal characteristic is a president invested with unlimited faculties and resources. This has converted him fatally into the Great Dispenser of Goods and Favors, even of miracles."[46] Valadés would seem to concur. Note Cosío's use of the qualifier "fatally."

## The Established Literature on the Mexican Presidency

What are the implications of the foregoing discussion of the Echeverría presidency for the conventional wisdom, that is, the established literature on Mexican politics by U.S. scholars? Surely one of the best-known North American writers in this regard is L. V. Padgett. The second edition of his widely used text says, "the president is a semidivine father figure to the people, inherently good in caring for his children. He is never directly challenged, as for example in the press, because that would shake the very basis of secular government."[47] Clearly, Padgett's vision is utopian in the light of the evidence presented earlier in this chapter. Yet, it is correct to say that the president may *try* to appear to be what Padgett says he is.

Each sexenio is prefaced with an extensive campaign in which the president-to-be tours every state in the country and uses surrogates to reach out to the villages (we noted earlier how this technique may appear an empty ritual to other Latin Americans). The conventional wisdom is that the president-to-be can probe public sentiment on key issues during his campaign tours, and better equip himself to reflect his nation's desires in the policy-making process he will later direct. True, as Valadés says, the president could do so—if he wanted to. Moreover, Cosío pointed to Echeverría's use of the watchword "autocrítica" as a pretense for turning self-criticism into a public function; however, as Cosío also noted, Echeverría's use of the term was inappropriate because the people were never really invited to criticize anything of substance.[48] Thus, the conventional wisdom about testing public sentiment via a grass roots campaign, especially when no real opposition is able to express itself, needs to be rethought.

Another piece of conventional wisdom is that the president must take an intermediate position between the official party's left and right wings, and that he can do so because there is a "core consensus of Revolutionary values" throughout all of the PRI.[49] This is probably still sound, albeit tenuous. To be sure, Echeverría clashed frequently with the powerful right-wing "Monterrey Group" in the area of national security policy and over the question of the government's expanding role in the economy. The Marxist review *Punto Crítico* referred to the Monterrey Group as the principal source of Mexican fascism, and cited conflicts that had grown during the Echeverría sexenio between the group's powerful families and the federal government over monopolistic control of the steel industry.[50] But the same source also pointed out the impressive amounts of state capital that had been loaned on favorable terms to the Monterrey Group as an appeasement device. It reaffirmed the idea that for the group's political influence to be effective it must operate within the PRI, not as in 1940, when certain members of the group supported the opposition candidate, Almazán, against the PRI's official candidate, Avila Camacho.[51] So it appears that, barring a complete rupture between the two, the group will remain a somewhat disaffected right wing, but well within the PRI's penumbra.

Selection of Treasury Secretary López Portillo to succeed to the presidency in 1976 may have done something to appease the PRI's political right. This would support the conventional claim that there is a core value consensus of sorts within the PRI. But it is questionable how far this applies to the disaffected left—to the growing alienation against the PRI's labor magnate Fidel Velásquez, led by Rafael Galván and others; to similar alienation against the agrarian sector of the PRI, led by Danzós Palomino and the *Central Campesina Independiente* (CCI), or to the congeries of guerrilla insurgents totally outside the "revolutionary coalition."

It has been argued that the institutionalization of the presidency has put a premium on "moderation and mildness in the political style" of the president as he seeks to balance competing interests and pressures.[52] Echeverría's forcing his attorney general and others to resign following the San Cosme scandal, his repeated but unfulfilled promises to disclose the true nature of the Falcons, his conflicts with the Monterrey Group and with the students of the National University, his intervention in Sonora over the Biebrich affair (for which he was partially responsible), and his subsequent takeover of *Excelsior* all suggest that Echeverría found moderation difficult, especially when he was challenged personally. The San Cosme affair was an especially bitter pill to take since even the establishment press of the capital city, normally loyal to the government in any dispute, criticized the PRI and laid photographic evidence at Echeverría's feet, demanding that he solve the problem of official terrorism (which, of course, he could not do in any real sense without losing face). It may be that the selection of López Portillo again reflects the perceived need to bring into the presidency an actor more prone to the moderate style that has lent stability to the institution in the past. Presidents beginning with Miguel Alemán in 1946 had been able to moderate conflict before it broke into open disorder, a skill less characteristic of Díaz Ordaz, and even less so of Echeverría.

Institutionally speaking, there is less need to modify the conventional wisdom. For instance, at the beginning of this chapter it was noted that much of the constitutionalism surrounding the presidency is mere formalism, given the near-absolute decision-making power that has accrued to the president. That is because his formal duties are sufficiently flexible to allow for wide interpretation regarding the accretion of power, among other things. The president has a wide variety of ceremonial functions that he can use for symbolic purposes as he chooses. He is commander in chief of the armed forces; in his final two years, however, some of Echeverría's public admonitions suggested a weakened confidence in his own control over the military. Also, most legislation is initiated by the president, and the congress is little more than a rubber stamp: there is, of course, no effective opposition in the congress. Insofar as justice is concerned, the Mexican president has considerable power to influence decisions of the judiciary via appointment of judges and by initiating removal proceedings in the congress. The president has enormous financial power over the states and localities via his control of grants-in-aid and because the central government has preempted most taxation prerogatives for itself. In the field of foreign affairs, on major questions, it is the president alone who decides, although normally his foreign minister will be consulted. Resignation of the foreign minister following the international reaction to Mexico's 1975 anti-Zionist vote in the United Nations makes one question whether Echeverría had undertaken consultation or not. The same question may be raised with respect to the breaking of diplomatic relations with Chile in 1974, an abandonment of Mexico's traditional commitment (the Estrada Doctrine) to recognizing new governments, whether de facto or de jure.

Probably the best way to summarize the importance, and complexity, of the president's power role is to depict him as the nerve center of a legion of demands by interest groups, regional political chieftans (or *caciques*), the three sectors of his party and their subsidiary organizations, the alienated satellite parties and "out groups," and a number of foreign influences (principally North American). As a nerve center, then, the president must moderate conflict and dispense a maximum number of "streams of satisfactions" in the hope of balancing competing interests so that the revolutionary coalition will not fall apart.

Compared to his predecessors, Echeverría may have had less "nerve center" capability, and the revolutionary coalition has, indeed, been threatened with atrophy during his regime. Yet, in all fairness to Echeverría, it may be that any other president would have fallen victim to the same dilemmas. With population pressure far outrunning economic expansion, and with less escape valve potential for desperate laborers north of the border, the pressures on the presidency are likely to grow. One must underscore the fact that the constellation of alienated groups beyond the penumbra of the PRI is growing because the party is unable to spread its largesse more effectively, due to increased demands. Defection is inevitable. This will put López Portillo's "nerve center" skills severely to the test during the 1976–82 sexenio.

## The Future

The future of the Mexican presidency may depend upon resolution of a key dilemma or paradox. This has been put well by Padgett; that is, the incumbent is supposed to accept responsibility for all that occurs within the system even though it is humanly impossible to oversee it all. Thus, Echeverría was sullied by the Biebrich scandal in Sonora. His "left leaning" toward Salvador Allende of Chile made Echeverría a target of attack by the Monterrey Group for having contributed to an atmosphere favorable to terrorism. The protesting students in March 1975 saw the president as the personification of Mexican fascism, and he accused them of the same thing. And Echeverría's last months in office—highlighted by the president's eleventh hour effort to distribute land—caused the specter of the military to assume a more active role in Mexico's political future. The list goes on ad infinitum. Padgett states the presidential paradox as follows:

> He is supposed to be a benevolent father. Whatever he does for the masses, he does for them personally—he endows them or gives them public structures, sanitation plants, schools, and roads. By the same token, if he fails to provide these things, he has failed in his vital fatherly role. *It is paternal government, but it is only legitimate if it is benevolent paternal government.*[53]

Obviously, with Mexico's socioeconomic sloth relative to her population pressure, and given competing intra-PRI demands for scarce resources, no president can avoid the wrath of the multitudes who are left unsatisfied. Some, like the poet-philosopher Oscar Monroy Rivera, will depict the president as one who must declare to the world what an exemplary place Mexico is, all the while enriching himself illictly and hiding his crimes. In a pejorative mood, Monroy has written about the imaginary country, Dwarfland (*Enanonia*), that is a transparent allegory for Mexico. Monroy sees Mexicans as dwarfs who are manipulated and exploited by a single-party political system whose principal norm is avarice. All and any who oppose Mr. President of Dwarfland are assassinated at the chief executive's command by militarists who use a controlled press to tell appropriate lies to the public.[54]

But there is always one great unknown that lingers, emerging from the instillment of that benevolent presidential father image in the popular mind, an image that the most humble have learned to invoke as a part of their socialization. This idea is exemplified by passages from a Mexican novel written by a federal deputy of the political opposition who once tried to help the poor of his region. Their struggle was for justice against the entrenched central party bureaucracy atop of which the president of Mexico sits. The novel shows the degree to which the mystique of an omnipotent, thaumaturgical, but benevolent president has been instilled into the minds of the humble masses, even of those who had been victims of the president's callous neglect. Pedro Alvidres, a peasant farmer, was driven from his land in Chihuahua by oligarchs of the PRI. He made the desperate illegal trek north of the border seeking work but fell into the hands of Mexican agents upon returning. His body was later found floating in the Rio Grande. Pedro was superstitious, yet religious, and held faith in witchcraft medicines and in mysterious revelations of divine truth. But Pedro, a typical Mexican poor devil or *móndrigo* (victim of society), believed in things even more absurd than those:

> He believed, for example, in honor, justice, . . . in love, in labor; he believed, ultimately, in a series of utopias, he had that great faith of the miner. But his belief was a pathology in itself, he was dead serious in putting it forth, serious in respecting the law that was in force, in giving an open road to nature's vital forces; he had faith also, an immense faith, in the benevolent justice of the President of the Republic.[55]

The great unknown, then, is how long Mexicans are likely to legitimize the system through their blind faith in a supernatural father figure—how many groups will decide that they are living in Enanonia, then organize outside the penumbra of the official party and rebel. Mexicans may not place their trust indefinitely in the "benevolent justice" of a president who distinguishes himself by gracing the international cocktail circuit, seemingly impervious to starvation and despair at home, and who then employs paramilitary squads and the army to silence those who bring him publicly to task. One day such a president may well find that he is seated atop the apex of nothing.

## NOTES

1. There is a recurring theme in Mexican politics wherein traitors to the official ideology of the single-party system are "executed" or sacrificed. An opposition deputy once wrote that whenever he would challenge the government on the floor of the Chamber of Deputies the essence of the rebuke he received would be "that Maximilian was shot in Querétaro and that no matter how many times it would be necessary there would be found another Hill of Bells (where Maximilian died) to execute other traitors" (my translation from Carlos Chavira Becerra, *La otra cara de México* [Mexico: La Nación, 1966], p. 20). Four years later, when the presidential succession was just beginning, the political cartoonist Abel Quezada picked up the same theme: "What do we call ideas which oppose the PRI? An exotic doctrine. And what do we have for those who preach exotic ideas? A Hill of Bells" (translated from his "Escalera de frases," *Excelsior*, 29 de marzo de 1970). For a discussion of the sacrificial priest or tlatoani tradition, see Octavio Paz, *Posdata* (Mexico: Siglo Veintiuno Editores, 1970).

2. See Frank Brandenburg, *The Making of Modern Mexico* (Englewood Cliffs, N.J.: Prentice-Hall, 1974), p. 141.

3. Evelyn P. Stevens, *Protest and Response in Mexico* (Cambridge, Mass.: MIT Press, 1974), p. 126.

4. A profound treatment of the national catharsis that Tlatelolco was and is today is found in the novel *La Plaza*, by Luis Spota (Mexico: Cuadernos de Joaquín Mortiz, 1972). A social science treatment written at the same time is Chapter 6 of Kenneth F. Johnson's *Mexican Democracy: A Critical View* (Boston: Allyn and Bacon, 1972).

5. Daniel Cosío Villegas, *El estilo personal de gobernar* (Mexico: Cuadernos de Joaquín Mortiz, 1974).

6. This contention is based on the author's extensive interviews plus accounts carried just after June 10, 1971, by the publications *La Batalla* and *¿Por Que?* The most thorough work on the event, which also credits Echeverría with responsibility for los Halcones, is Gerardo Medina Valdés, *Operación 10 de junio* (Mexico: Ediciones Universo, 1972).

7. *Excelsior,* 2 de abril de 1976.

8. Ibid.

9. *Visión,* 1 de mayo de 1976, p. 14.

10. The problem of human displacement into the United States would be a critical and delicate issue for the next Mexican president, José López Portillo, to deal with. Some dimensions of the problem are treated in Thomas Weaver and Theodore E. Downing, eds., *Mexican Migration* (Tucson: University of Arizona Press, 1976).

11. See Kenneth F. Johnson, *Guerrilla Politics in Argentina* (London: Institute for the Study of Conflict, 1975). A part of Echeverría's condemnation of the Argentine military is contained in *Excelsior,* see note 7, above.

12. New York *Times* editorial, July 13, 1976. See also an article in the Washington *Post* by Terri Shaw, July 14, 1976, that credits the takeover of *Excelsior* to both Echeverría and his former secretary, Fausto Zapata, who was in the process of building a media empire for Echeverría to use in perpetuating his rule once out of office. Significantly, the chief of *Excelsior*'s Washington Bureau, Armando Vargas, stated that the future president López Portillo was a distant blood relative of *Excelsior*'s ousted director, Julio Scherer García, and that the president-elect would most likely turn out to be another Cárdenas in the sense of undoing some of his predecessor's deeds. Thus, there was some hope that the new sexenio (1976–82) would see renewed freedom of the press in Mexico, but this would depend almost entirely on the character of López Portillo as political actor. Should he prove to be unable to accept public criticism, as was Echeverría, there would be little likelihood of change.

An additional note on the takeover of *Excelsior* is that Echeverría prevented news coverage of this action in Mexico. By and large, Mexicans had to learn of it from the outside. According to Armando Vargas' testimony communicated to this writer, Echeverría even threatened Julio Scherer García with the charge of treason if he accepted an invitation to speak in New York about the *Excelsior* affair: the latter is said to have declined for fear of his own safety. One of the more bitter ironies is that in 1971, at the beginning of his sexenio (and two days before the San Cosme massacre of protesting students), the president addressed the press corps on "The Day of Press Freedom" and declared "when governments assume that the state is infallible they lay the basis for dictatorship" (*Excelsior,* 8 de junio de 1971).

13. "Los ritos electorales," *La Opinión,* (Buenos Aires), 4 de junio de 1976.

14. Ibid.

15. Cosío, *La sucesión presidencial* (Mexico: Cuadernos de Joaquín Mortiz, 1975), p. 144. See also Philip Agee, *Inside the Company: CIA Diary* (London: Penguin Books, 1975), p. 509.

16. Cosío, *El estilo personal de gobernar,* op. cit., p. 13.

17. Cosío, *La sucesión presidencial,* op. cit., pp. 144–45.

18. Ibid., p. 18.

19. Ibid., p. 145. It bears repeating the belief in some Mexican sectors that López Portillo might turn out to be another Cárdenas and undo much of the legacy of his predecessor.

20. One of many examples of formally published affirmations that Moya Palencia would succeed Echeverría is found in Gastón Rivanuva R. (pseudonym), *El PRI: El gran mito mexicano* (Mexico: Editorial Tradición, 1974), p. 79. There is always the possibility that this very publication was a "trial balloon" sponsored by the government to test reaction to Moya Palencia and to gauge reaction to a number of regime abuses cited therein. Part of the psychology of the Mexican presidency, as told to this writer by informants well located in the presidential secretariat, is to use pseudonyms under which deliberately disparaging commentaries are published about the

regime to create the facade of "revelations" about which the government is not afraid and can correct. A pseudonym can always be discredited, however—not so with *Excelsior,* where editorial responsibility was clearly fixed.

21. See Cosío, *La sucesión: desenlace y perspectivas* (Mexico: Cuadernos de Joaquín Mortiz, 1975), passim.

22. Ibid., pp. 94, 103.

23. *La Batalla* (Mexico City), mayo de 1975.

24. *El Imparcial* (Sonora), 26 de octubre de 1975.

25. Based upon this writer's interviews with colleagues from Sonora during 1976, and also on the account given in *Onda* (Sinaloa), 12 de noviembre de 1975. The account by *Onda* also involves governor Biebrich and Moya Palencia in the international narcotics traffic.

26. Document in this writer's possession (*Consignación,* Hermosillo, Sonora, 20 de enero de 1976). This is a legal indictment prepared by the Sonora government's attorney general *(procuraduría general de justicia del estado de Sonora).*

27. *Excelsior,* 15 de marzo de 1975. See especially testimony on p. 12–A. Considering that Echeverría came to power with the image of "the new and younger generation" it is strange that some of his worst problems were with students. Echeverría had served briefly as a law professor at the National University (UNAM) in 1947. When he was being promoted through the tapado ritual and groomed for the presidency, the Young Revolutionary Economists of Mexico (a subgroup of the PRI's popular sector, or CNOP [Confederación Nacional Obrero Patronal]) produced a brochure extolling Echeverría's dedication to youth called "Ideario político y social," Mexico, 1969 (mimeograph). This was the early image Echeverría gave to the outside world, that is, that of being for the "new generation in a country where 60 percent of the population is under 20 years of age" (from Jean-Claude Buhrer's article reproduced from *Le Monde Diplomatique* (Paris) by *Excelsior,* September 17, 1972).

28. *Excelsior,* 15 de marzo de 1975.

29. As quoted in Johnson, op. cit., p. 164.

30. See José C. Valadés, *El presidente de México en 1970* (Mexico: Editores Méxicanos Unidos), pp. 51–52.

31. Ibid., p. 55.

32. Ibid., p. 74.

33. Ibid., pp. 82–83.

34. Ibid., pp. 100–02.

35. Ibid., p. 125.

36. Ibid., p. 148.

37. In the 1976 elections the PRI broke almost a half-century tradition. It allowed Jorge Cruickshank, leader of the Popular Socialist party (PPS) to win a Senate seat from Oaxaca state. Reportedly, this was to compensate for the fact that a PPS candidate for the governorship of Nayarit had been the victim of official fraud the previous year. Cruickshank, as leader of his party (which traditionally endorsed the PRI's presidential candidate), mediated the dispute, which could have grown to public proportions and would have seriously embarrassed the PRI (according to an account in the St. Louis *Post-Dispatch,* July 18, 1976). The results of the 1976 election gave to the PRI 194 seats in the Chamber of Deputies, 19 to the PAN, 9 to the PARM, and 8 to the PPS, thus assuring the PRI's hegemony once again. According to this writer's testimony, the PAN and the PPS would undoubtedly have won more seats had it not been for widespread electoral fraud.

38. Valadés, p. 150.

39. According to a letter written to this author by Raúl González Schmal, one-time provisional president of the PAN and a high-ranking member of his party's hierarchy, the PAN suffered a severe internal crisis during 1975–76 and ultimately decided to abstain. This is discussed at great length in the writer's "Opposition Politics and the Future of Mexico," a chapter in a forthcoming

book to be published by the University of Arizona in collaboration with the Center for Latin American Studies at Arizona State University.

40. Stevens, op. cit., p. 259.

41. Cosío, *El estilo personal de gobernar,* op. cit., pp. 49–50.

42. In all fairness to Echeverría, one must cite as examples of attempts during his regime to deal with poverty and economic stagnation such ventures as SICARTSA (state sponsored steel production) and INFONAVIT (public housing for workers). Their impact remains to be seen.

43. Cosío, *El estilo personal de gobernar,* op. cit., p. 57.

44. Ibid., p. 58.

45. Ibid., pp. 60–62.

46. Ibid., p. 128.

47. L. V. Padgett, *The Mexican Political System* (Boston: Houghton Mifflin, 1976), p. 187.

48. Cosío, *El estilo personal de gobernar,* op. cit., pp. 112–14.

49. Padgett, op. cit., p. 196.

50. *Punto Crítico,* primera quincena de julio de 1976, p. 18.

51. Ibid.

52. Padgett, op. cit., p. 197.

53. Ibid., p. 214 (emphasis added).

54. Oscar Monroy Rivera, *El señor presidente de Enanonia* (Mexico: Costa-Amic, 1973), p. 43. My translation and paraphrasing.

55. Carlos Chavira Becerra, *La otra cara de México* as cited in Johnson, op. cit., p. 96. To a certain extent the accretion of power in the U.S. presidency, as revealed by the Watergate and intelligence investigations, tells the story of the enormous centralization of power in the Mexican presidency, but in Mexico the press and congress are helpless.

CHAPTER

# 4

**COSTA RICA:**
**THE SHRINKING OF**
**THE PRESIDENCY?**
Kenneth J. Mijeski

## INTRODUCTION

"Costa Rica has lived in peace. One enjoyed liberty in Costa Rica. . . . In the hurricane of dictators and disturbances, Costa Rica was an oasis . . . 'the Switzerland of Central America; the country with more teachers than soldiers.' "[1] Such has been the nature of much of the published literature on Costa Rica, which has not-too-subtly characterized that country as the contemporary pinnacle of democracy in the southern part of the Western Hemisphere. Politically speaking, it is quite clear that Costa Rica, like most other Latin American countries, has a presidential rather than a parliamentary form of government. Moreover, and once again like her sister Latin republics, a good portion of this constitutional presidential system was styled after the structural aspects of the Constitution of the United States.

Given the above tentative characterizations of Costa Rica as a constitutional presidential democracy, how might we, in closer examination, depict the actual functioning of the presidential system? Not being a parliamentary system, how does it operate? What role does the president play in the Costa Rican presidential system? Does the chief executive simply carry out policies developed and passed by the legislature? Or is the president of Costa Rica, like Clinton Rossiter's U.S. president, also his government's chief legislator? Is he, like most of his Central American counterparts, a dictator in democrat's clothing? Or, on the contrary, is he a sadly weakened administrative clerk overwhelmed and manipulated by a powerful legislature and a burgeoning, uncontrollable bureaucracy? The central purpose of this chapter is to sketch at least some preliminary answers to such questions. To begin this task, we should first turn to a more general, albeit brief, depiction of political history in order to provide a context within which to better understand the functioning of this particular political institution.

The colonial experience of Costa Rica differed significantly from that of her immediate neighbors, and Latin America in general. By and large, Costa Rica escaped the plunder and pillage, and subsequent militarization and violence, endured for hundreds of years by other parts of the Spanish New World. In large part, there was good reason for the lack of plunder: Costa Rica did not have the riches so eagerly sought by the conquistadores. There was no overabundance of gold for the Spanish coffers nor for the Church's buildings. Nor were there sufficient quantities of Indians available to work as slaves on the fertile lands of the central plateau. Therefore, as Alberto F. Cañas put it, "The Spaniard who came to Costa Rica had to come as a colonist and not as a conqueror; to live and not to grow rich."[2]

This did not mean that the colonial and early postindependence periods were free from internal discord and the politics of violence. The nineteenth century, for example, had its share of the typical Latin American *cuartelazos* (military uprisings) and military-style dictators. Cañas, however, in his generally sympathetic treatment of Costa Rican history, argues that most of the dictators were possessed of a "spirit of progress and republicanism."[3] Moreover, in contrast to other parts of what was to become Central America, the political path of Costa Rica was comparatively peaceful. A tradition of peaceful transfer of power between presidential administrations became the norm rather than the exception.[4]

What were the extent and scope of presidential power in the postindependence period? One recent study concluded that prior to the 1940s the locus of power resided in the presidential office, particularly in the personality of the president.[5] The congress was expected to be subservient to the wishes of the executive, especially since it was the president who largely determined who would become a deputy in the congress.[6] Nevertheless, there were still scattered reports of legislative restrictions on presidential activities as far back as the 1800s. For example, Carlos Monge Alfaro noted that President José Rafael de Gallegos (1833–35) had to obtain congressional permission to visit his ranch just a few miles outside of the capital city.[7]

Even into the early 1940s the office and personality of the president seemed to predominate in making important policy decisions. In the second year of the administration of Rafael Angel Calderón Guardia (1940–44), for example, the congress began a custom of approving the budget of the previous year, but giving the executive the liberty to implement any additions that the president and his ministers considered necessary. Moreover, it seemed to be the rule that the congress would approve with virtually no discussion the majority of bills initiated by the executive branch.[8] The last year of Calderón Guardia's administration, on the other hand, makes it clear that presidential decision making was checked in some areas of policy making: when the president decreed amnesty for some of his followers who had been found guilty of electoral offenses and fiscal infractions, the Supreme Court declared those decrees to be unconstitutional.[9]

This action by the Supreme Court was one among several, both legal and extralegal, that were to result not only in severe restrictions of presidential authority in the long run, but would also culminate in the so-called revolution of 1948, the only instance in modern Costa Rican history where more or less peaceful and constitutional settlement of disputes gave way to overt violence.[10] Policies and personalities emerged during and after the revolution that were to have critical implications for presidential decision making. The self-named "Generation of 1948," the prime movers of the revolution, included several young men who were to rise to national political prominence. The Generation includes, for example, the "father" of modern politics in Costa Rica and two-time president, José "Pepe" Figueres Ferrer, and one of his comrades-in-arms, Daniel Oduber Quirós, who was to become a deputy in the Legislative Assembly and to succeed to the presidency in 1974. The 1948 war and subsequent events may be viewed as a climax to the Costa Rican tendency to fear any concentration of power in the executive arm of the government. One observer argues that this tendency is a "Costa Rican tradition that can be traced back to the earliest days of the republic."[11]

In the broad context of Latin American politics it is nonetheless ironic to suggest that the major perpetrators of the revolution proposed and enacted policies designed to weaken rather than enhance executive authority. Yet, this appears to be precisely what has occurred on two levels: a conscious, rational level; and a level of unplanned, largely unintended, consequences of otherwise rational decisions.

The remainder of this chapter will more closely scrutinize political events in the post-1948 era and their impact on the development of the decision- and policy-making roles of the presidency. We will examine the constitutional aspects of the postrevolutionary period as reflected in the virtually rewritten constitution of 1949 and some critical amendments that have subsequently been made, and how these rational, carefully planned efforts have had profound and unforeseen consequences on the ability of contemporary presidents to govern. In addition, an analysis will be made of the party system and the impact of personal characteristics of some recent presidents within that context.

## CONSTITUTIONAL ASPECTS OF PRESIDENTIAL POWER

The groundwork for the new constitutional order was begun during the reign of the postrevolutionary junta headed by Figueres. Figueres' role, both ideologically and otherwise, was of paramount importance.[12] His views regarding the depoliticization of government work and the consequent establishment of a series of autonomous and semiautonomous institutions have had lasting repercussions. Under the constitution of 1949, the president was specifically assigned only four independent functions: appointment and removal of ministers; service as commander in chief of the *Guardia Civil* (remnants of a military force in Costa Rica after Figueres had disbanded the military on December 4, 1948, in an action unique in Latin American politics); representation of the nation at official ceremonies; and presentation of a state of the union address before the congress.[13] These unilateral functions make him anything but "all-powerful."

Additionally, the president was stripped of his previously broad-ranging authority to issue *decretos con fuerza de ley* (decrees with the force of law).[14] It should be pointed out that the president has limited authority to issue decrees that fall within the scope of existing laws. Several members and former members of the National Assembly, however, have expressed to the author the view that there have been several instances in which the president issued decrees that exceeded the scope of legislation already passed.[15] We have no systematic data regarding the extent to which this practice has occurred, though the author previously estimated that it may be fairly widespread.[16]

Although the president has the right of veto, he lacks an item veto and is even prohibited from exercising his blanket veto of legislative proposals without the concurrence of at least one of his cabinet ministers. Another unique part of the constitution, yet another check on presidential decisional authority, is the fact that the Costa Rican president is the only chief executive of a Latin American country who plays no role whatsoever in the selection of Supreme Court justices. They are appointed by the National Assembly, Costa Rica's unicameral legislature.

Of critical importance to any contemporary chief executive is the role he plays in the formulation and enactment of the national budget. Here again, the framers of the 1949 constitution, partly as a reaction to the previously mentioned budgetary practices of Calderón Guardia's administration, placed strict limitations on the president's role. To be sure, only the executive can initiate budget bills and the legislature is prohibited from increasing the budget (unless it can demonstrate a source of revenue to finance the increase), but the National Assembly is able to modify, within the general parameters set by the executive, any or all parts of the bill. Moreover, the definitive ability to approve or disapprove the final figuring of the budget explicitly resides in the legislature.

In the original constitution of 1949 the president was prohibited from seeking immediate reelection, just as the prerevolutionary president had been. Not at all unique in the Latin American area, this meant that every president would be a lame duck throughout his term in office. A recent amendment, however, made the duck almost dead: no reelection under any circumstances.[17]

As in the United States, moreover, the Costa Rican president plays no authoritative role in the amendment process. Although the legislature is required to submit a proposed amendment to the president for his comments, the deputies are under no obligation to accept any modifications the president may offer. The president cannot veto any amendment, or part thereof, to the constitution once it has been approved by two-thirds of the membership of the National Assembly.

In sum, the Costa Rican constitution is a document that apparently goes significantly beyond the checks and balances of a constitution such as that of the United States. It therefore reinforces the impression that one major upshot of the revolution of 1948 was a carefully planned attempt to prevent the possibility of inordinate power flowing from the executive office. But what has this implied in practice? Does the other side of the ledger describe, in contrast, a legislative body that has molded, coaxed, and coerced the executive branch to suit its own purposes? Since the National Assembly is a unicameral body of small size, it would seem that, without the added hindrance of an additional chamber, the legislature could strengthen its efforts vis-a-vis the office of the president. In actuality, for constitutional and other reasons, this has not clearly been the case.

## PRESIDENTIAL POLICY MAKING: SOME UNFORSEEN CONSEQUENCES OF POLITICAL EVOLUTION

### Legislative Dominance

In a pioneering study, Christopher E. Baker found that, at least in terms of initiating legislation, the National Assembly accounted for 72 percent of all bills initiated during an eight-month period;[18] furthermore, among those bills that could be categorized as important, the legislature also dominated the initiation phase.[19] Baker's study, however, suffered the limitations of a very short time period, so it would be premature to conclude that the president was indeed succumbing to the dominance of the legislature.

In fact, Baker's findings and general conclusions were modified in a broader study by Steven Hughes and this writer that encompassed a 12-year period and three presidential administrations: Mario Echandi (1958–62), Francisco Orlich (1962–66), and José Joaquin Trejos (1966–70).[20] An effort was made to examine policy making in terms of four analytically distinct stages: initiation, modification, acceptance-rejection, and review. The general conclusion from the research was that neither the executive nor the legislature is overwhelmingly dominant in making public policy. While the National Assembly, in support of Baker's findings, initiated the majority of all types of legislation, the executive branch got a slightly greater percentage of its bills passed with little modification than did the legislature. In the 12-year sample, approximately three times as many legislature-sponsored bills as executive-sponsored proposals suffered rejection, primarily at the hands of the legislature itself. Basically, a fear of presidential usurpation of power combined with a general tendency to opt for a broad checks and balances system seems to have resulted in a policy-making arena, here defined in terms of laws, where neither the executive nor the legislature is dominant.

Giving additional support to this conclusion, in a study of the entire political system, Charles F. Denton argues that:

> Despite its apparent powers the National Assembly is as limited as is the president in its ability to carry out its functions. The fact that the deputies cannot seek reelection until a four-year term intervenes tends to limit the continuity of the body and discourages specialization in particular policy-making areas. The committee system, with its revolving membership, assures that most issues will be acted upon in a piecemeal fashion and on the basis of limited information.[21]

## Autonomous Agencies and Decentralization

Another constitutional provision, brief and seemingly of little import, has had exceptional and far-reaching consequences for presidential leadership in the making of public policy. We refer here to Title Fourteen of the constitution of 1949, which calls for the creation of autonomous and semiautonomous institutions. The Figueres-led interim junta of 1948 set precedents by establishing the first two of these institutions, one being the country's banking system, which was entirely nationalized within the authority of an autonomous agency. Additional autonomous institutions, such as the social security agency *(Caja Costarricense de Seguro Social),* were created by the constitution itself. As delegated by the constitution, however, the legislature has been entirely responsible for the proliferation of these institutions, which now number about 130.[22]

The sizable number of these largely independent institutions was part of what we called the rational, carefully planned design of the revolutionary leadership. Figueres himself later noted that in 1948 he consciously opted for the then decentralized state model of Uruguay in order to limit the power of the president.[23] The constitution not only made these institutions autonomous in their day-to-day operations, it also provided for the presidential appointment of directing boards with staggered terms that would overlap with alternate presidential administrations, thereby effectively eliminating a spoils system as well as inhibiting presidential oversight of the institutions' practices. Moreover, in several cases the autonomous institutions design, implement, and raise the revenues for their own budgets, independently not only of the presi-

dent but of any other branch of government. In other instances, such as with
the Caja Costarricense de Seguro Social, the constitution specifies budgetary
minimums (in percentages) below which the central government may not
decrease the share of the economic pie to the autonomous agency. And even
in those cases in which an autonomous institution has to wrangle for an
unspecified share of the national budget, the wrangling takes place not with
the office of the president but with the office of the *contraloría general* (roughly,
the director of the bureau of the budget) who is appointed by and answerable
to the National Assembly.

There has been a growing awareness on the part of presidents since the
1960s, including Figueres, that this conscious effort at decentralization has
unintentionally resulted in the virtual inability of the president, as political
leader, to guide government problem solving. Figueres and other spokesmen
of the National Liberation party (*Partido Liberación Nacional* [PLN]) have
come to feel that new problems—rising unemployment, population growth,
and urbanization, among others—have presented new challenges to government and that the design of the present system was really adequate only for
meeting some of the old problems, such as communism and political corruption, over which the revolution of 1948 had been fought.[24] Since there are so
many institutions independently performing multiple functions, many of
which overlap or duplicate the functions of the bureaucracy of the centralized
sector, a problem of presidential authority arises:

> [I]f the central government turns over its economic powers to decentralized
> agencies, its own *técnicos* remain in a position which is relatively powerless.
> If economic expenditure plays a more dynamic role in national development
> than social and administrative outlay, the president has little leverage to
> change the direction of his country's affairs.[25]

## Attempts to Restore the Balance

Has anything been done to rectify this problem of the weakening of
presidential authority? In 1968 the National Assembly modified Article 188
of the constitution of 1949 to permit autonomous agencies to enjoy the right
of administrative independence, but *not* the right of making their own policies
independently of the executive or legislative branches. But this amendment
may have more symbolic than tangible impact on policy making because, as
the Contraloría General reported in 1967, "the inevitable limitation of personnel prevents a complete and permanent control of public administration; therefore, it is possible only to make selective and periodic checks" of certain
institutions.[26]

More recently, at the initiation of Presidents Figueres and Oduber, the National Assembly passed two laws that attempted to return some authority over the autonomous institutions to the president: the so-called "4-3 law" passed during the 1970–74 Figueres administration, which gave the incumbent chief executive a majority on the boards of the semiautonomous institutions; and the law passed during the Oduber administration, which gave the president a 7-0 majority on the governing boards of these institutions.[27] It is probably too soon to evaluate the long-run effects of these new laws on presidential authority. But for the present, the problem still remains: how can the president, as the most visible political leader, assert himself in a situation that has been characterized as "political immobilism"?[28]

## POLITICAL PARTIES AND PRESIDENTIAL STYLE

### Historical Background

The "modern," mass-based political parties discussed in contemporary political science literature were nonexistent prior to the revolution of 1948. As in most Latin American nations, Costa Rican parties were highly personalistic in nature, with virtual absence of any systematically organized mass following.[29] This is not meant to imply that modern parties emerged full-blown after the revolution. On the contrary, even the PLN, the closest thing to a "developed" party, was, at least at the outset, simply a vehicle for the personal ideological ambitions of José Figueres and his followers. This association was to persist into the early 1970s, such that the man-on-the-street would be equally likely to identify himself as a *figuerista* or a *liberacionista*. In any case, the PLN is the dominant party in what has been variously called a modified two-party system[30] and a modified two-party system that may be moving toward a multiparty system.[31]

### Interparty Power Struggles

These characterizations bear some analysis relative to their importance for presidential policy making. The leadership and dominance of the Figueres-inspired PLN has created a context since 1953 in which non-PLN parties have taken an essentially oppositional, defensive posture. For example, as often as not the campaign rhetoric of non-PLN parties has emphasized what has been wrong with PLN programs.[32] Unfortunately, from the perspective of their electoral prospects, precisely what is wrong with the PLN receives varied and often contradictory emphasis from opposition parties as widely divergent as Manuel Mora's Social Action party *(Partido Socialista* [PASO] the current modified version of the old Soviet-line *Uanguardia Popular)* and the conservative, occasionally reactionary, National Union party (*Partido Unión Nacional* [PUN]).

This has meant that in only two of six presidential elections since 1953 have the opposition parties been successful at the polls. Moreover, the opposition parties have succeeded only once in denying the PLN a majority, albeit at times a slim one, in the 57-seat National Assembly.[33] Thus, one would expect that PLN presidents would have had significantly greater success in policy making vis-a-vis the legislature than non-PLN presidents, especially given the description of the PLN as a highly disciplined congressional party.[34] From previous research using aggregate data, this has not been the case.[35] Ironically, the opposite has been true (see Table 1).[36] Although the sample size is small and the conclusions are, therefore, tentative, PLN President Orlich accounted for a slightly greater proportion of all bills defeated during his term in office than did either Echandi or Trejos.

## TABLE 1
### Bills Defeated (by administration, in percent)

| Sponsor of Bill | Echandi (non-PLN) | Orlich (PLN) | Trejos (non-PLN) |
|---|---|---|---|
| Legislature | 76.4 | 71.4 | 79.5 |
| Executive | 23.6 | 28.6 | 20.5 |
| Total | 100.0 (55) | 100.0 (42) | 100.0 (39) |

$X^2 = .254$   $p \leqslant .90$

## The Presidency of José Joaquin Trejos

What the data do not demonstrate is the particularly bitter fighting that has characterized disputes between non-PLN presidents and the PLN-dominated National Assembly. For example, President José Joaquin Trejos, a mathematics professor without previous political experience, perhaps won a pyrrhic victory in capturing the presidency in 1966 with the support of the National Unification party, a sometimes coalition of the old party of Calderón Guardia, the National Republican party and the previously mentioned PUN, founded by Otilio Ulate. A good portion of Trejos' campaign took the form of attacks upon his liberacionista opponent, Daniel Oduber, whom Trejos accused of having procommunist leanings. These attacks on a respected leader of the PLN left that party, which controlled the National Assembly, in a nonconciliatory mood. This mood was soon felt by Trejos when he sent the 1967 budget to the legislature.

For years, the PLN-dominated assembly had practiced a policy of deficit financing of the national budget through the use of both domestic and foreign loans. One negative result was the creation of a very heavy burden of debt service on these loans. In an attempt to rectify this situation, Trejos' budget proposal included a 5 percent sales tax and a land tax. Immediately, the liberacionista deputies criticized the taxes as regressive and unfair and then proceeded to slash away at the budget, eliminating the entire funding for every embassy in South America, leaving only three embassies in all of Europe, and heavily reducing the funds for the Washington embassy. Through intense efforts at negotiation, these harsh measures were modified and the compromise budget did include a small sales tax. But the lesson was clear: an inexperienced non-PLN politician must be careful in his attacks on his PLN rivals, even when he has won the presidency.

## The Presidency of Mario Echandi

On the other hand, a seasoned politico can be a minority president, clearly oppose PLN policies, and, to some extent, get away with it. Such a president was Mario Echandi. Much more politically experienced than Trejos, his National Unification party successor to the presidency eight years later, Echandi came from a very political family. His father, Alberto, was himself president of the republic in the 1920s. Echandi became secretary-general of the PUN in 1947 and, in 1948, directed the presidential election of Otilio Ulate. In 1950 Ulate appointed him ambassador to the United States and he was named foreign minister in 1951. He was elected in 1953 to the National Assembly, in which he was an active leader of the opposition parties. The vigor with which he opposed the PLN-controlled chamber led to his being indicted for treason for his sympathy for the abortive invasion attempt staged by the exiled Calderón Guardia in 1955. He was suspended from the legislature, but was successful in getting the indictment dropped and later resumed his assembly seat.

His outspoken oppositional style and his successes and bitter struggles prepared him well for the presidency. He used the veto more than any contemporary president, and with more success. In the first ten months of his administration he vetoed 18 PLN-sponsored bills and was overridden only once. This is not to say that he, as a minority president, was completely successful. It is to say, however, that a seasoned, outspoken politician like Echandi is capable of slowing down somewhat the legislative dominance of the PLN. During his administration, for example, central government intervention in the economy was curbed and no economic development programs were initiated.[37]

## The Presidency of José Figueres Ferrer

What happens to the power of the president when he not only is the founder and avowed leader of the dominant party in the National Assembly but when, additionally, his style is flamboyant? In recent times, only one president can be thus categorized, José ("Don Pepe") Figueres Ferrer. Much has been written by him and about him: a few examples that demonstrate his flamboyant style and his only slightly limited ability to influence friends and foes alike, both within and without the presidential office, follow.

Figueres is one of two modern presidents who has captured the masses. The other was the late Calderón Guardia. This writer recalls one evening several years ago in a downtown San José movie theater when a newsreel showed Don Pepe touring Spain. In a Spanish automobile factory, always playing to the camera, he determinedly kicked the tires on the assembly line, supposedly testing their mettle. At a historic site, Figueres outrageously struck a pose of a nearby statue with arms and legs askew. The burst of warm, affectionate laughter from the audience was unbelievable. Here was Don Pepe, at once the old *patrón,* the father figure, and the chief executive of a modern nation state playing the buffoon for his "children."

A different facet of his flamboyance was the much-reported hijacking attempt in 1971. A hijacked Nicaraguan airplane had requested and received permission to refuel at San José's Juan Santamaría airport. When Figueres got word of the happenings, he jumped into his limousine, drove onto the landing ramp of the airport, borrowed a submachine gun from an airport guard and proceeded to riddle the plane and its tires with bullets. The hijacker surrendered and President Somoza of Nicaragua sent his personal thanks to Don Pepe.

But does this public style facilitate translation to political decision making? The answer appears to be in the affirmative. Figueres carries in his political baggage innumerable assets that would be envied by any politician: identification with the masses; a near-legendary reputation stemming from his unique political skills exhibited before, during, and after the revolution of 1948; and recognition as founder and indisputable leader of the party that has dominated Costa Rican politics for over 20 years.[38] Moreover, Figueres often appears to be an influential policy maker whether or not he is actually the president. In the above-mentioned budget dispute between President Trejos and the National Assembly, one source characterized Figueres as the key figure in facilitating some working agreement.[39] As PLN leader, he could afford to criticize the legislature's moves as "demagogic," while at the same time declaring his hostility to Trejos' proposed land tax in a country with so many small farmers.

Another critical policy that sheds light upon the personal capabilities of Figueres was the Protocol of San José. By the late 1960s the balance-ofpayments difficulties in Central America had become a central concern of the various governments. President Trejos made a commitment at a meeting in El Salvador to try to get a measure approved in Costa Rica to meet this problem. Then the economic ministers of the Central American nations, with the exception of Panama, met at San José and drew up the protocol, the major feature of which was a 30 percent surcharge on duties on imports from outside the Central American region. The aim was to curb the consumption of imported luxury goods and some raw materials.

The National Assembly, again through *liberación* leadership efforts, repeatedly balked at ratifying the measure.[40] Figueres wished to run for the presidency in 1970, but was being challenged for his party's nomination by Rodrigo Carazo, a deputy in the legislature and an opponent of the protocol. Figueres was known to favor the protocol but maintained a low profile in that regard, in light of the intraparty struggle. There were even charges from the opposition that the liberacionistas were purposely dragging their feet on ratifying the protocol until after their party's presidential nomination was decided.[41] The protocol, in any case, was never ratified during the Trejos administration. Once Figueres won both his party's nomination and the election, he made his position regarding the protocol known. This time, with the support of the National Assembly's PLN membership, the Protocol of San José was finally ratified in 1970.

Even in situations where the cards seem stacked against him, Figueres somehow emerges the victor, at least in terms of maintaining control of the legislative wing of his party. One such example concerns the well-known Vesco-Figueres linkage. Politicians of both the ruling and opposition parties, civic leaders, intellectuals, and some businessmen have joined forces in efforts to achieve the deportation of Robert L. Vesco. Rodolfo Solano, a leader of the National Assembly's PLN delegation, pointed out the dangers of Vesco's presence in Costa Rica: "In a small country Vesco's economic power translates into political power. In the future, he may play a key role in political decisions, helping elect deputies or even a president."[42] Nevertheless, just before surrendering the reigns of government to his protege, Daniel Oduber, Figueres initiated a bill to reform the extradition law that would make it difficult, if not impossible, to obtain Vesco's extradition.[43] With Figueres conveniently out of the direct limelight, President Daniel Oduber has had to bear the brunt of the public outcry over the Vesco case.

## The Presidency of Daniel Oduber

Oduber's style is in marked contrast to that of his predecessor and mentor. Where Figueres plays the crowd, Oduber prefers to play politics quietly. He has gained a reputation as a good negotiator and a talented arm-twister in the

National Assembly, in which he served as president from 1970 to 1973. He has been known to defer to Figueres on occasion. Before the Vesco-Figueres linkage was known, Oduber saw no problem at all in getting Vesco extradited. After the connection became public in 1973, Oduber was conspicuously silent, perhaps being aware that his ambitions for the presidency, once thwarted at the polls (Oduber had been a PLN presidential candidate in 1965), would fall flat without the endorsement of Don Pepe.

President Oduber's administration marks a precedent. It is the first time the PLN has succeeded itself in the presidency. Given the adherence of Oduber to the PLN mainstream and given Figueres' role as an advocate, rather than as a "loyal opponent," Oduber's tenure should be marked by presidential effectiveness in policy making. On the other hand, Oduber's electoral victory was hardly a mandate, with around 43 percent of the vote. Moreover, he lacks a clear PLN majority in the National Assembly, having to rely on splinter party votes to obtain a working majority.

At least one event has occurred during his tenure in which he could draw upon Costa Rica's nonpartisan, reawakening sense of nationalism: the scandal in which United Brands Company was allegedly involved in bribing government officials in Honduras and Costa Rica in order to secure lower export taxes on bananas. Oduber threatened to send a bill to the National Assembly canceling the operation contracts of the company's Costa Rican subsidiary and banning its operations permanently if it failed to reveal the names of the Costa Rican officials involved in the alleged bribery deal.

## SUMMARY AND CONCLUSIONS

The Costa Rican presidency is a study in paradox. Although in many respects the Costa Rican presidential system is modern and institutionalized, it is nonetheless subject to extreme personalism, such as that of José Figueres. And while an erstwhile president and full-time politician like Figueres can and does assert inordinate influence upon the political decision-making process, he himself was the key architect of a constitutional structure that virtually locked the doors against freewheeling presidential power. The Costa Rican political system is like others, both historical and contemporary, that have made it the business of legislatures to act as watchdogs over presidential excesses. As we have seen, however, the legislature itself, with its inadequate research staff and the constitutional provision for no immediate reelection, is already overburdened with other tasks.

As regards institutional power, we have witnessed the development of scores of autonomous and semiautonomous agencies. These have become the functional equivalent of a fourth branch of government, further robbing the contemporary presidency of the ability to respond vigorously to changing national problems. These agencies portend more than just a diminution of presidential power, as economist Dennis J. Mahar points out:

> The primary danger involved in the decentralization of national government is not so much that it dilutes the power of the president (although this may produce serious difficulties in the promotion of national planning), but that it provides a "back-door" method of greatly enlarging and fragmenting the public sector. As mentioned above, it often becomes difficult to dissolve these "states within states" . . . once they are created. Thus after a period of rapid decentralization, a country finds itself with a Frankenstein which is very difficult to destroy, i.e., hundreds of autonomous agencies competing for revenues (with each other and with the national and subnational governments), duplicating functions, and possessing no real common goal other than self-preservation and/or some dim concept of "national development."[44]

The greater the extent to which these agencies proliferate and have the ability to define and act upon their own concepts of national development, the greater the problem of political accountability becomes. For at least two presidential administrations the voters have thrown out the PLN rascals, and occasionally given them a tough time in the National Assembly. But how can a president, of any party, be held responsible for the activities of institutions created by the legislature ten years earlier, the governing boards of which are dominated by appointees of his predecessor in his first (and therefore last) term of office?

The flamboyant president exhibits a facade of assertive authority in dealing vigorously with plane hijackings and scandals perpetrated by individuals in collusion with "Yankee" corporations. But the verdict is not yet in on the ability of the contemporary Costa Rican president, borrowing another of Clinton Rossiter's phrases, to serve as a clear and strong beacon of national purpose.[45]

## NOTES

1. Alberto F. Cañas, *Los ocho años* (San José: Editorial Liberación Nacional, 1955), p. 7. This and all translations, unless otherwise noted, are by the author.

2. Ibid.

3. Ibid., p. 9.

4. For a good, single-volume account of this and other developmental patterns, see Carlos Monge Alfaro's *Historia de Costa Rica,* 9th ed. (San José: Imprenta Trejos Hermanos, 1959).

5. Robert D. Tomasek, "Costa Rica," in Ben G. Burnett and Kenneth F. Johnson, eds., *Political Forces in Latin America: Dimensions of the Quest for Stability* (Belmont, Calif.: Wadsworth, 1968), p. 110.

6. Ibid.

7. Carlos Monge Alfaro, op. cit., pp. 156–57.

8. Oscar R. Aguilar Bulgarelli, *Costa Rica y sus hechos políticos de 1948* (San José: Litografía Lehmann, 1969), p. 84.

9. John Patrick Bell, *Crisis in Costa Rica: The 1948 Revolution* (Austin: University of Texas Press, 1971), p. 73.

10. Probably the best descriptive account in English of this period is ibid.

11. James L. Busey, "Costa Rica: A Meaningful Democracy," in Martin C. Needler, ed., *Political Systems of Latin America* (New York: Van Nostrand, 1964), p. 123.

12. For a good, general statement of José Figueres Ferrer's political, social, and economic ideology, see his *Cartas a un ciudadano* (San José: Imprenta Nacional, 1956).

13. For these provisions and others discussed herein, see *Constitución Política de la República de Costa Rica* (San José: Imprenta Nacional, 1970).

14. This presidential prerogative is fairly common in Latin America and was widely used, for example, by Chilean Presidents Eduardo Frei and Salvador Allende when confronted by powerful legislative opposition to their programs. This type of decree authority, which the Costa Rican president does not possess, essentially bequeaths to the president the unilateral capability to make laws.

15. Kenneth J. Mijeski, "The Executive-Legislative Policy Process in Costa Rica" (Ph.D. dissertation, University of North Carolina at Chapel Hill, 1971), pp. 127–29. A more condensed and overtly comparative version is in Steven W. Hughes and Kenneth J. Mijeski, "Legislative-Executive Policy-Making: The Cases of Chile and Costa Rica," *SAGE Research Papers in the Social Sciences: Comparative Legislative Studies Series,* No. 90-007 (Beverly Hills: Sage, 1973), esp. pp. 18–20, 38–39.

16. Mijeski, op. cit., p. 129.

17. Former Presidents José Figueres and Mario Echandi were permitted to run in the 1970 elections because a clause in the amendment exempts from the provision all presidents who held office prior to 1966.

18. Christopher E. Baker, "The Costa Rican Legislative Assembly: A Preliminary Evaluation of the Decisional Function," in Weston Agor, ed., *Latin American Legislatures: Their Role and Influence* (New York: Praeger, 1971), pp. 53–111.

19. Ibid.

20. Hughes and Mijeski, op. cit., esp. pp. 28–40.

21. Charles F. Denton, *Patterns of Costa Rican Politics* (Boston: Allyn and Bacon, 1971), p. 38.

22. Costa Rica, Dirección General de Estadística y Censos, *Anuario Estadístico* (San José: Imprenta Nacional, 1968), pp. 306–07.

23. From interviews with José Figueres, cited in James W. Wilkie, "Recentralization: The Budgetary Dilemma in the Economic Development of Mexico, Bolivia, and Costa Rica," in David T. Geithman, ed., *Fiscal Policy for Industrialization and Development in Latin America* (Gainesville: University Presses of Florida, 1974), p. 204.

24. Ibid., p. 229.

25. Ibid., p. 232.

26. Costa Rica, Contraloría General de la República, *Memoria Anual,* 1968, 1-B, quoted in Wilkie's chapter in ibid., p. 235.

27. Charles F. Denton, "Costa Rica's Human Resources, Politics, Population and Change" (unpublished manuscript, 1976) chap. 3, p. 47.

28. Charles F. Denton, "Bureaucracy in an Immobilist Society: The Case of Costa Rica," *Administrative Science Quarterly* 14 (1969): 418–25.

29. Bell, op. cit., esp. pp. 3–19. Note, however, the proliferation of party labels even before the 1949 revolution. The Communist party *(Vanguardia Popular)* was perhaps the only ideologically organized party at that time.

30. Baker, op. cit.

31. Robert H. Trudeau, "Costa Rican Voting: Its Socio-Economic Correlates" (Ph.D. dissertation, University of North Carolina at Chapel Hill, 1970), pp. 201–10.

32. See Denton, *Patterns of Costa Rican Politics,* op. cit., pp. 54–66, for a description of the various parties. The 1974 presidential elections have even seen the addition of a few more anti-PLN parties: the Democratic Renovation party, the National Independent party, and the miniscule Democratic party.

33. The PLN became a minority party after the 1974 elections, with 27 of the 57 seats. Although the PLN did not, by itself, hold the majority of the seats in the legislature during the Echandi presidency, the PLN leadership could regularly count on enough splinter party votes to constitute a working majority.

34. See, for example, Denton, *Patterns of Costa Rican Politics,* op. cit., p. 61.

35. Hughes and Mijeski, op. cit., esp. pp. 34–37.

36. Adapted from Ibid., p. 36.

37. Denton, *Patterns of Costa Rican Politics,* op. cit., pp. 32–33.

38. Only once in recent years was Figueres' leadership role seriously disputed. In 1970 Rodrigo Carazo, chairman of the National Assembly's Economic Affairs Committee, challenged Figueres for the PLN presidential nomination. Carazo lost.

39. New York *Times,* December 25, 1966, p. 23.

40. For some PLN arguments against the protocol, see Asamblea Legislativa, exposiciones del diputado Lic. Carlos José Gutiérrez del Partido Liberación Nacional, *Protocolo de San José,* sesiones plenarias, enero 1969.

41. Ibid.

42. New York *Times,* February 16, 1975, p. 27.

43. Ibid.

44. Dennis J. Mahar, "Comment" to James W. Wilkie, in Geithman, op. cit., p. 253.

45. Clinton Rossiter, *The American Presidency,* rev. ed. (New York: Mentor Books, 1960), p. 250.

# 5

## THE COLOMBIAN PRESIDENCY: CONTINUITIES AND CHANGES
### Robert H. Dix

Political scientists have traditionally divided the world's constitutional systems into presidential and parliamentary types. Of the two, Latin American political systems fall clearly into the former category with but fleeting and partial exceptions. Yet, as Jacques Lambert suggested some years ago, Latin American polities are really best classed in a third category, that of presidential dominance,[1] since at least in practice they eschew the sort of balance of power among the three separate branches of government that characterizes the archetypical case of presidentialism, that of the United States.

Colombia has largely shared that pattern of presidential dominance, despite some periods of attempted executive constraint. Generally speaking, the president's formal and informal strength has been far greater than that of Congress or the judiciary, while departmental (state) and local governments have in the last analysis been dependent on him. At the same time, the Colombian president, in company with other Latin American presidents, has been severely circumscribed in his power, especially by the phenomenon we shall call "the weak state." In fact, the limits on presidential domination have been historically greater in Colombia than in almost any other Latin American country. The nature of these limitations, and the reasons for them, will therefore be worth some particular attention.

Dominant, therefore, in comparison to the other institutions of government (though less so than in other Latin American cases), yet traditionally weak in its ability to effect policy and carry out its decisions, the Colombian

The author would like to thank Andrés Moreno for his insightful comments on the draft of this chapter.

presidency has undergone some important changes over the course of the last 40 years, and notably since the late 1960s, that suggest that the presidency is becoming both stronger and more dominant. Yet, this new dispensation remains in a kind of dynamic tension with the politics of the past. Upon the nature of their interaction depends the future of both the presidency and constitutional government in Colombia, as well as the prospects for the pursuit of development goals.

## THE ROOTS OF PRESIDENTIAL POWER

The difference between presidential dominance and a presidential system like that of the United States is of course a distinction of degree rather than of kind, and subject to the variations of presidential personality and political circumstance. Nevertheless, presidential dominance is manifest in the very authority which the Colombian constitution (in common with most other Latin American constitutions) grants the chief executive.

In the first place, his appointive powers are much more extensive than in the case of the U.S.-style presidency. The president can appoint cabinet ministers and many other high officials without the approval of either house of Congress. Since the system of government is unitary rather than federal, the president appoints the departmental governors (who in turn appoint the mayors of municipalities), thus giving the president direct or indirect control over positions high and low throughout the national, departmental, and even municipal bureaucracies. Because state intervention in the economy and in other aspects of national life (for example, education) is extensive, the president also has appointive authority, either directly or through his ministers or governors, over such positions as the rectors of most of the nation's universities.

The authority to issue decree-laws, or decrees with the force of law, is likewise considerable. Thus, Congress is given the authority, not infrequently exercised, to grant the president extraordinary powers for specified periods "when necessity demands it or the public convenience advises it" (Article 76). In addition, it is common practice for Congress to pass laws in quite general terms, thus granting to the president unusually broad power, in North American terms, to implement the legislation as he sees fit. The executive's powers are further enhanced by his constitutional authority to declare certain matters "urgent," thus requiring priority congressional attention (Article 91); and by the stipulation that cabinet ministers shall participate in congressional debates (Article 134). In fact, most legislation of national importance originates with the executive, even though bills of congressional origin slightly predominate quantitatively.[2]

Provision for the presidential assumption of extraordinary power in crisis situations is also a prominent part of the Colombian constitution.[3] Thus,

Article 121 permits the president to declare the public order disturbed in all or part of the country and to issue the requisite decrees, as well as to suspend, though not rescind, existing laws. Every administration since World War II has found it necessary to invoke a state of siege over all or part of the country; it was most recently invoked, from June 1975 to June 1976, by President Alfonso López Michelsen in the wake of a series of guerrilla raids and urban kidnappings. As former President Alberto Lleras Camargo (1958–62) lamented, "Everything of importance for the citizenry, both in the way of fundamental norms and in social and economic matters has almost without exception been the product of extraordinary faculties authorized by the Congress to the executive or of decrees under the state of siege."[4]

A final major constitutional basis of presidential authority rests with his control over the budget. The president has the item veto, and in 1968—a few scant years before the powers of the U.S. Congress were being strengthened with regard to the budget—the budgetary controls of the Colombian Congress were being weakened.

In short, in such crucial areas as appointments, decree-laws, emergency powers, and the budget, the Colombian president clearly has greater authority within his political system than the U.S. president has within his.

The real sources of presidential power in Colombia, nevertheless, lie deeper than constitutional authority. One such source is Colombian political culture. Thus, Reid Reading has argued that early socialization patterns place constraints on the extent to which Colombians perceive the relevance of impersonal institutions for problem solving and task management. Reading interprets this finding to partially explain the relative weakness of Congress and the comparative strength of the obviously more personalized presidency in Colombia.[5] The frequent personalization of political factions (*lleristas, lopistas, laureanistas,* and *ospinistas* are examples) is further evidence of the same phenomenon. A certain tendency toward *caudillismo* thus has deep cultural roots. In fact, the entire patrimonial tradition inherited from the Spanish colonial system, including its emphasis on administrative and civil law, provides the cultural and historical underpinning for the nature of the country's republican presidency. The prevalence of the status incentive among Colombian politicians, which among other things has the effect of fostering factionalism, high turnover rates, chronic absenteeism, and inefficient work habits among legislators, similarly strengthens the presidency by weakening the effectiveness of Congress as an institution.[6]

Perhaps even more important are the structural reasons for presidential dominance. In Colombia, as in most so-called developing societies, the budget of the central government and the jobs which government can provide are critical to the well-being of a great many people. In a society where status has traditionally accrued to governmental rather than commercial employment, where socially acceptable jobs in the private sector have (at least until recently) not been very numerous, and where the system of spoils and patronage prevails, the president's constitutional authority in these areas looms as that much more important.[7] The fact that such societies are relatively so vulnerable or dependent on the international environment, and on economic and other factors beyond the confines of their own boundaries, similarly gives the government, and with it the chief executive, an unusually critical role. In short, in developing societies generally, where other structures or networks of relationships are weak or inadequate to integrate the society, the president as head of government tends to assume an importance relative to other institutions, and even a domination over them, that is less pronounced in the so-called more-developed nations.

The fact that the president is commander in chief of the armed forces and of other security services is yet another source of presidential power. To be sure, constitutions in any presidential system, including that of the United States, customarily give the president this authority. The distinction in the Colombian and comparable Latin American cases is that the armed forces, by custom and function, play a different role than they do in North America. Except nominally, they have usually played an insignificant role in external defense. Rather, their preeminent role has been one of internal security. Thus, as long as the president can retain the political loyalty, or at least neutrality, of the military—and most especially if the country is under a state of siege and some of the normal constitutional inhibitions on governmental action are suspended—he has a weapon that can be formidable indeed. This has been particularly evident in the Colombian case over the last 30 years, when politically derived violence has seemed almost endemic.

There are, then, a variety of factors, reflected in the provisions of the Colombian constitution and deeply rooted in the political culture and nature of the political system, that help to make the Colombian presidency predominant among the institutions of government. Many of these factors are similarly evident in other Latin American countries, where presidential predominance is also the norm. This much being said, Colombia differs from much of the rest of Latin America in being historically a country where there have been more constraints on presidential power than in most others. The reasons for this tell us a good deal about the Colombian presidency in its contemporary, as well as in its historic, manifestations.

## LIMITS ON PRESIDENTIAL POWER: COMMONALITIES

There are, to begin with, some constraints on their power that Colombian presidents in essence share with their Latin American counterparts. They include certain constitutional and institutional checks; the influence of economic associations, and of such institutions as the Church and the armed forces; public opinion as reflected in elections, the press, and even protest demonstrations; and the phenomenon that we shall refer to as "the weak state."

## Constitutional and Institutional Checks

The constitution prescribes a sharing of power with a bicameral congress and a judicial branch. Above all, the Colombian Congress has often been able to delay, reject, or otherwise thwart the legislative initiatives of the president —although it has seldom been able to exercise that initiative with regard to major legislation. Thus, Congress was able to stall a major agrarian reform bill, finally passed late in 1961, for almost two years, and to do much the same with respect to the 1968 constitutional reform. It has so far frustrated attempts at a comprehensive urban reform, despite the efforts of several presidents. Moreover, Colombian congressmen have been quite effective in representing the particularistic interests of their regions and in obtaining the corresponding perquisites for their constituents.[8] President Carlos Lleras Restrepo (1966–70) remarked at one point that: "Not one single executive bill has been passed by Congress, while in four months of government I have had to sign numerous regional aid laws . . . which if totaled up would represent the national budget for ten to twenty years."[9] As congressmen themselves see it, it is not through the drafting of legislation, but by means of citations to cabinet ministers, committee investigations, congressional debates, control over the budget, and the amendment or rejection of executive proposals that they exercise their influence over the executive.[10]

The economic associations that probably have the most influence on presidential actions and policy are the Federation of Coffee Growers (*Federación de Cafeteros* [FEDECAFE]) and the National Association of Manufacturers (*Asociacón Nacional de Industriales* [ANDI]), although the gamut runs from associations of cattlemen, bankers, rice growers, engineers, and merchants to the two principal national labor confederations, the Union of Colombian Workers (*Unión de Trabajadores de Colombia* [UTC]) and the Confederation of Colombian Workers (*Confederación de Trabajadores de Colombia* [CTC]).

FEDECAFE has a special, institutionalized role. Although it is essentially a private association of coffee growers and traders, by law several government officials sit on its national committee and its manager is appointed by the president of the republic from a list submitted by FEDECAFE's national congress. The manager in turn acts as Colombia's representative in international negotiations concerning the coffee market, while FEDECAFE acts in an official capacity to set coffee prices and regulate exports. FEDECAFE's role is exceptional and is obviously a reflection of the centrality of coffee to the well-being of the entire country. Other interest associations, however, play institutionalized roles of a lesser nature—for example, by being accorded by law a position on the boards of directors of such government agencies as the Colombian Institute of Agrarian Reform (*Instituto Colombiano de Reforma Agraria* [INCORA]). Less formally, but nonetheless importantly, Colombian presidents have been known to call national conferences of the *fuerzas vivas* (that is, the most important groups, including business and labor organizations) to recommend policy. The proposals of such a commission were in fact used as the basis for a series of bills submitted by the government to Congress in 1965. The agrarian reform bill presented by the president to Congress in 1960 was also a direct product of a blue-ribbon commission composed of political and interest group leaders.

## Interest Groups

Access of interest groups, it should be noted, is much more often sought and obtained through the executive branch of government than tends to be the case in the United States, in yet another indication of presidential dominance. Nonetheless, the ease of such access should not be exaggerated, despite what has already been said.[11] For there is some evidence that, at least for the past decade, Colombian interest groups are finding effective access more difficult in the wake of the increasing prominence of technocrats in certain key institutions of the executive branch, particularly those concerned with economic policy and planning.

In any case, the behavior of most interest groups toward policy proposals put forward by the executive seems to be primarily reactive and defensive. For example, in the case of a 1969 urban reform bill, it was not until the project had received the unanimous approval of a congressional committee that concerned groups showed enough interest to organize an ad hoc group of "lawyers and bankers of firms specializing in real estate" to resist its passage.[12] When protests against government actions are denied, groups not infrequently take direct action in the form of strikes or boycotts. The latter are by no means limited to the ranks of students or labor. Although exceptional in its objectives and its consequences, the civic strike that helped to overthrow General Gustavo Rojas Pinilla in May 1957, which included the voluntary closing of many banks and businesses, was a notable example of direct political action on the part of some of the more powerful Colombian interest associations.

It is worth a comparative note that organizations reflective of popular interests, such as those of workers or peasants, have been relatively ineffectual in Colombia, despite the perceptions of congressmen, who rank the UTC and the CTC fourth and fifth, respectively, in terms of their influence on Congress.[13] Although the CTC has always had certain ties to the Liberal party and the UTC was founded as the result of Jesuit instigation, none of the country's labor confederations has developed the kind of institutionalized position that marks Venezuelan or Mexican politics; nor, it seems fair to say, do they have equally effective access to the presidency. Organizations of *campesinos* or *usuarios,* formed a decade ago essentially to provide a popular rural base for the government and its rural programs, became radicalized and have subsequently become "marginalized" from access to the president. Peasants, in fact, never have had a major input into Colombia's agrarian reform programs.[14]

## The Church

The Roman Catholic Church is probably as politically influential in Colombia as in any country of the world and its wishes must be taken into account by any president. Until quite recently the Church tended to identify its secular fortunes with the Conservative party, and it was common practice to denounce Liberals as heretics. The Church was therefore a formidable antagonist for most Liberal presidents; in the case of the Conservatives it often had a voice in the selection of the party's presidential candidate.[15] In recent decades the Church has sought a more neutral role, however, and it has been a staunch supporter of the bipartisan coalition that has governed Colombia since 1958. Its prelates have even appeared on campaign platforms on behalf of Liberal candidates. Meanwhile, the Church retains an effective veto power over areas of vital concern to it, such as education and divorce. Although in 1974 President Alfonso López Michelsen, a Liberal, was able to get through Congress a species of divorce bill in line with a campaign promise, Church opposition ensured that it would be very limited in its application, allowing divorce only to those married outside the Church, and thus to only a tiny minority of Colombians.

## The Armed Forces

The armed forces, though a distinct asset to a president who retains their loyalty, may also pose severe constraints on presidential action and, of course, may well threaten his very tenure. Significantly, few Colombian presidents have been overthrown by the military. Moreover, the minister of defense, customarily a military man in most Latin American countries, was often a civilian. Although in recent decades the ministry of defense has always gone to a general, presidents have on several occasions been able to dismiss the minister, or the commander in chief of the army or of the armed forces, when he threatened to become too enmeshed in politics or was too overtly critical of the government. President Valencia did so in 1965, President Lleras Restrepo in 1969, and President López Michelsen made a similar move in May 1975.

With the onset of endemic violence in the late 1940s, however, the army became increasingly involved in combat against the guerrillas. Indeed, the attempt on the part of President Laureano Gómez to use the army for partisan purposes was a major factor in the military coup that overthrew him in 1953. It meanwhile became frequent practice to name military officers as departmental governors in regions of particular violence, and the military was used on at least one occasion to occupy the oil camps and the city of Barrancabermeja during a petroleum workers' strike. In sum, the military can be said to have an effective veto power over presidential action in the field of internal security, as well as an important voice in matters affecting frontier areas, the national territories, and certain aspects of foreign policy.

## Public Opinion

As in any political system where elections are in some sense meaningful, public opinion also constrains the president or, on the contrary, affords him opportunities. Thus, following his near defeat by an urban-based populist (the former dictator, General Gustavo Rojas Pinilla) in the presidential election of 1970, the new president, Misael Pastrona Borrero, began actively to promote a program of urban reform, as he did once again prior to the midterm elections of 1972. Following the latter election, and with the progovernment candidates generally victorious, this interest in urban reform waned once again and an activist minister of economic development was removed from office.[16] Again, the presidential election of 1974 gave the Liberal Alfonso López Michelsen 56 percent of the vote and what even Conservatives acknowledged to be a *mandato claro* to pursue his proposed program. On the other hand, the intractability of the problems facing any president, particularly under conditions in which he still had to share office with the other party, made some of López' inevitable failures that much more glaring and productive of dissatisfaction.

## The Weak State

Perhaps most importantly, Colombian presidents have shared with their Latin American colleagues the incubus of a weak state. That is, however strong the president might be relative to Congress and the judiciary, his ability to effect his will, especially in the sense of carrying out general policies, has been considerably weaker than might be supposed. It is in this sense that a U.S. president is usually stronger than a Latin American president, even when he is less dominant.

There are several aspects of this weakness. Poor communications, high rates of illiteracy, and the like mean that many rural areas, in particular, are not effectively penetrated by the agencies of the central state and may have only a tenuous connection to it. Agency bureaucracies tend to be inefficient, while resources, and therefore budgets, are often inadequate to meet basic needs.[17] Meanwhile, a culture that stresses patron-client relationships and particularistic favors makes it difficult to carry out general policies and to establish the state as a neutral enforcer or arbiter above the claims of individual interest or access. The fact that the bureaucracy is essentially chosen by the spoils system is another aspect of the same phenomenon. Also, Colombian presidents, like other Latin American chiefs of state, must function in an international environment of great powers and of economic forces over which they can exert little influence. Actors such as foreign governments, international banks, and transnational corporations—the decisions of which have a very important impact on Colombian prosperity and even, potentially, on the survival of a government—are substantially, albeit not entirely, outside the control of any president. Thus, Richard Nelson et al. declare that "the operation of constraints or pressures external to the policy-making system [appears] to be the key element in provoking recent major policy changes in Colombia," citing as instances a set of tax and administrative reforms put through in 1962 and a wholesale revision of foreign exchange policy in 1967.[18]

For such reasons, and others analogous to them, the Colombian state has in the past tended to be weak, even when its presidents were dominant figures within their own governmental framework.

## LIMITS ON PRESIDENTIAL POWER: DIFFERENCES

Colombian presidents share many constraints with other Latin American presidents, although the particulars naturally differ. Notably, mass organizations such as labor unions and peasant groups are less important in Colombia than in, say, Venezuela, while the Church has probably been more significant politically, and the armed forces less so, than in most of Latin America. Still, the relative historic weakness of the Colombian president in comparison to the great majority of his Latin American colleagues remains to be accounted for.

### A Distinctive History

As a matter of fact, the evidence is quite clear that presidential dominance has been less the case, generally, in Colombia than elsewhere. Outright dictatorship, which might well be viewed as the nonconstitutional extreme of presidential dominance, has been rare in Colombia. Thus, there have been only

four real dictatorships in Colombian history—those of General Rafael Urdaneta (1830–31), General José María Melo (1854), General Rafael Reyes
(1904–09), and General Gustavo Rojas Pinilla (1953–57)—all of them quite
brief. Such regimes as that of General Tomás Cipriano de Mosquera (1861–63)
and Laureano Gómez (1949–53) might also be thought of as quasi-dictator-
ships, but again they were few and brief. None, military or civilian, has ever
taken on the dimensions of the rule of Juan Vicente Gómez (Venezuela) or
Porfirio Díaz (Mexico).[19] For a time, indeed, during the nineteenth century,
Colombia experimented with one of the most decentralized federal systems
ever to exist in Latin America, with presidents limited to two-year terms in
order to contain their power.[20]

The corollary of such a record has been the unusual extent to which
Congress has historically been able to resist the presidential will. The principal
parallels in Latin America would be pre-1973 Chile, Costa Rica, and pre-1967
Uruguay. Such a role for Congress, and the relative absence of dictatorship,
has been grounded in the persistence of a meaningful political opposition
during most of Colombian history. True, there have been long periods when
one or the other historic party—the Liberal or the Conservative—has governed hegemonically, without effective challenge from the other; only occasionally has one party given way to the other as the result of free elections.
Yet there have been a few such occasions, 1930 and 1946, for example: this
phenomenon has never yet occurred in Mexico and did not occur in Venezuela
until 1968. Given the intense nature of party loyalties (the so-called hereditary
hatreds) in Colombia, there was always a residue of articulate opposition that
was difficult for any president to repress or co-opt, and ready to take advantage
of any presidential faltering or, more likely, any division in the governing
party.[21]

A final kind of evidence of the constraints on presidential power in Colombia comes from a series of provisions and arrangements—some of them
embodied constitutionally, others informal—which have sought to limit that
power. These include, for example, very careful attempts to surround the state
of siege by such safeguards as the requirement for ministerial counter-signa-
tures on decrees, the prohibition against the repeal of prior legislation, and (by
a 1960 amendment) a stipulation that Congress shall be able to send any decree
issued under the state of siege to the Supreme Court for a determination of its
constitutionality. Such limits, as a rule, have been more explicit than those of
other Latin American constitutions.[22]

## Interparty Coalitions

More unusual and more significant, however, have been the interparty
coalitions created to share power between the Conservative and Liberal parties. They have usually required that the president divide his cabinet among

representatives of the two parties and thus have given the opposition party a kind of veto power through its representatives in the cabinet. Such coalitions tend to come into being at moments of crisis. Twentieth-century examples include: the Republican Union of 1910, which followed shortly upon the War of the Thousand Days and an ensuing dictatorship; the National Concentration of 1930–34, which was formed to effect the transfer of power from the Conservatives to the Liberals; the National Union of 1945–49, which had a sporadic existence in the late 1940s at the time of another crisis in the party system; and the National Front of 1958–74, which was formed in the wake of years of partisan violence and military dictatorships. The last of these has been by far the most elaborate of such arrangements and its essence was incorporated into the constitution during the late 1950s. Its principal provisions included parity between the Liberal and Conservative parties in all legislative and appointed posts below the presidency, alternation of the presidency between the parties every four years for a period of 16 years, and the requirement of a two-thirds vote to pass congressional legislation.[23] The National Front has been a signal success in accomplishing its intended purposes of preserving the political peace and preventing the return of dictatorship.

Such coalition agreements between the parties—and they have occurred quite frequently throughout the last century or more of Colombian history— obviously diminish presidential freedom and flexibility in the critical area of his appointive powers, as well as in policy formulation. No other Latin American country, with the sole exception of Uruguay and its *coleqiado,*[24] has taken such extensive and elaborate measures to guard against one-man and one-party rule.

## Civilian Elites

Of central importance in the explanation of this relative weakness of an independent executive has been the historic strength of Colombia's civilian elites, reinforced perhaps by their regional dispersion. Even today, Colombian presidents tend to be selected from a very narrow social stratum, with the social ties and dependencies that that implies. Thus, among Colombia's post-1958 presidents, four out of five were at the time of their election long-standing active or honorary members of Bogotá's exclusive Jockey Club.[25]

As early as the independence and immediate postindependence periods it was clear that these elites would be able to rein in the ability of an armed caudillo to control the country.[26] There were of course numerous regional strongmen who came to the fore in the first half-century or so of Colombian history, and a few succeeded in winning the presidency—José María Obando, Tomás Cipriano de Mosquera, and José Hilario López come to mind. Yet, their rule was invariably short-lived, and the majority of Colombian presidents have been civilian "aristocrats"—lawyers, intellectuals, and/or members of established landholding or merchant families—rather than "men on horseback" in the tradition of Venezuela's José Antonio Páez or Mexico's Santa Anna. The fact that, given the country's balanced regionalism[27] and the difficulties of internal communication, it was difficult for any central government genuinely to control the entire country made it quite easy for dissidents to challenge the rule of any president. To survive in office a president had to have at least the acquiescence of a significant number of regional leaders. The counterpart of such rule, what Gino Germani has called limited participation aristocracy, was naturally the weakness of the military, which, as already noted, has historically been less prone to seize power in Colombia than it has elsewhere in Latin America.[28]

## Party Factionalism

The chief mechanisms of elite influence have been the two historic parties and their various factions. Here again the Colombian political system is somewhat exceptional in the Latin American context. The continuity of the parties is marked; their roots go back more than a century. The intense loyalties that have been built up around them during this time span—both among elites and the masses—have given them a durability and a significance with which any president must reckon. The factional leaders of the parties tend to own the country's leading newspapers, and thus have a significant influence on public opinion. Those same leaders usually make the decisions that largely govern the congressional behavior of their members and that affect the degree of opposition a president will confront at other levels of government as well.[29] It is even within the parties' power to mobilize armed resistance to a president (or support for him). Nor does a president necessarily control his own party (and certainly not all factions of it), so opposition may come from that quarter as well. In short, without the acquiescence of the top party leadership it is difficult even today for any president to accomplish very much.

The party or factional leaders and directorates, most of them products of a narrow social stratum, pose the main limits to presidential power in Colombia—not the Congress per se, nor the restrictions of the constitution, nor even interest groups of different kinds. The president must therefore be constantly aware of factional interests, and must be able to thread his way among various demands, which often consist of concerns for jobs or factional advantage rather than sharp policy differences. In fact, even with at least the nominal support of major political factions, the two strongest, most reform-minded presidents in modern Colombian history—Alfonso López Pumarejo (1934–38 and 1942–45) and Carlos Lleras Restrepo (1966–70)—have both had to threaten resignation, and thus a crisis in the system, in order to get key legislation passed. López in fact lost his political balance during his second term and and felt impelled to resign.

If one were to generalize about the historic role of the Colombian president, one would thus have to conclude that his role in relation to other governmental institutions had been predominant, while at the same time his power was constrained (as was that of other constitutional chief executives in Latin America) by certain legal limits, the demands of powerful economic interest groups, the entrenched positions of such traditional institutions as the Church and the military, the weight of public opinion, and, above all, the overall weakness of the governmental machine, including its international dependency. All this being said, the Colombian presidency has been among the weakest in the hemisphere, and among the least inclined to dictatorship, in large part because of the way civilian elites have managed the unusual and tenacious party system.

## TRENDS IN PRESIDENTIAL POWER

Changes are under way, however, and have been for about the last 40 years. They have become even more evident within the last decade. These tendencies, hardly restricted to Colombia, though perhaps more noticeable there because of the unique political environment, encompass both the strengthening of the presidency and the development of a stronger state.

### The Expansion of Presidential Authority

Beginning in the 1930s, the role of the Colombian president began inexorably to expand as a result of the increasing functions ascribed to the central government in the fields of economic development and social welfare. Much of this change depended on presidential initiative, notably that of Alfonso López Pumarejo during his first administration (1934–38). Thus, the constitutional codification of 1936 formally accorded the state a role in economic development and gave it the legal means to protect both industry and consumers. The same set of amendments declared property to have a social function and to be expropriable under certain conditions, thus laying the basis for such subsequent executive-promoted measures as agrarian reform.[30]

The next several decades saw the role of the chief executive in economic and social matters grow apace, but the constitutional reform of 1968 was to be the next watershed in the growth of presidential power. Strongly promoted by President Carlos Lleras Restrepo, this reform signalled a marked shift in the legal basis of the balance of power between Congress and the executive. That the Congress would itself accept such changes—and that its preoccupations during the extended debate over the reform centered around certain electoral arrangements having to do with the prospective phasing out of the National Front rather than around the alteration in that balance[31]—says a great deal about the realities of power in the Colombian system. A constitutional revision such as that of 1968 would be unthinkable, certainly, in a presidential system such as that of the United States. Above all, the 1968 reform was the institutionalization of an established trend toward an increasing central government role in economic planning. What the reform did was to narrow the difference between the norms of the system and its actual behavior.[32]

Thus rewording and repositioning of several clauses of Article 76 (which enumerates the powers of Congress) altered rather explicit congressional controls over the budget, the national debt, and credit to more general and vague supervision with such wording as "to stipulate the general standards which the government must follow in. . . ." Again, congressional authorization of specific public works was eliminated and a more general supervisory clause substituted; the result was to weaken one of the congressmen's principal claims to the support of their local constituents.

Perhaps as important as any of the other 1968 changes was the provision for the declaration of economic emergencies (Article 122). In part at least, the design was to separate such emergencies from those covered by the provisions in Article 121 for the state of siege—in the preceding two decades a state of siege had often been invoked to meet economic crises, in a manner presumably unintended under an article dealing with public order.

The new article had the effect of explicitly legitimizing the president's authority to legislate by decree in economic emergencies, and specified that such decrees could repeal or modify existing law.[33] President López Michelsen was to invoke Article 122 in order to enact a major tax reform in 1974. On the other hand, despite threats to do so, his predecessor did not invoke it to enact a promised urban reform.[34]

Clearly, therefore, a Colombian president must still mobilize political support to pursue policy initiatives; the 1968 reform is not sufficient to permit arbitrary rule on his part. With a mandato claro immediately behind him, López Michelsen could put through extensive tax reform by using Article 122; with a more tenuous base of support, plus the reactive opposition of various political factions and interest groups, President Misael Pastrana Borrero (1970–74) failed to push urban reform, despite his averred support of it. Nevertheless, most observers, as well as many congressmen, seem to agree that the reform of 1968 marked a signal decline in the power of the legislature and a corresponding increase in the legal basis of presidential authority.[35]

Meanwhile, the stipulated 16 years of the National Front have come to an end, and with them some of the limitations on presidential power. In fact, the original provision of the coalitional agreement, that most legislation would require a two-thirds congressional majority, had already been reduced to the customary simple majority by yet another part of the 1968 reform. The end of presidential alternation has eliminated that restriction of the president's influence on the choice of his successor. Although parity in appointive posts is to persist until 1978, thereafter the president will be free of partisan limitations on his appointive powers, except for the vague proviso that he give "adequate and equitable participation" to the principal opposition (or nonpresidential) party.[36] Of course, at the same time, the formal end of coalition deprives the president of a kind of institutionalized bipartisan support.

## The New Technocracy

The presidency has been strengthened as well by a development of an altogether different kind: the growth of a group of technocrats (*técnicos*) who in recent years have come to staff such important government organs as the National Planning Department, the Monetary Council, and the Colombian Institute for Agrarian Reform (*Instituto Colombiano de Reforma Agraria* [INCORA]). These técnicos have goals and attitudes that contrast markedly with those of most Colombian politicos. The goals of the technocrats tend to be development and policy enactment, not partisan or factional enhancement. They provide a reservoir of expertise that enhances presidential capabilities in such complex areas as modern economics and that both supports and helps generate presidential initiatives in areas of social reform. In some ministries and agencies, at least, they tend to form a kind of barrier between the demands of interest groups, the more politically attuned ministers, or the president himself.[37]

Thus, whereas the Colombian Banking Association used to largely dictate monetary policy, "it now faces the hermetic Monetary Council which is not in the least interested in consulting with it concerning the measures it plans to enact." The same student of Colombian pressure groups further comments that "some presidents of influential interest associations have been forced to resign because of their growing inability to communicate with certain government offices." He concludes that:

> Pressure organizations have found it increasingly difficult to penetrate some of the new bureaucratic organs. The entire phenomenon of the transfer of power to the executive and the creation of technocratic structures, from which the President and his Cabinet get their advice, have been a formidable obstacle for the maintenance of access. Moreover, the great importance attributed to centralized planning in the design of public policy has undoubtedly contributed further to isolate government from the representative [interest] associations and even the private sector as a whole.[38]

The president is in one sense strengthened by such technocratic trends. He may also become more isolated from political realities. Thus, when President Lleras Restrepo attempted to promote an urban reform bill in 1966 he found that the legislation had little support among politicians or key interest groups. It had apparently been developed by técnicos in the Ministry of Economic Development without any real effort to marshal political support or even to consult others who might be concerned with the matter.[39]

Concomitant with the growth of technocracy has been the increasing institutionalization of the office of the presidency itself. Bodies such as the Department of National Planning and INCORA are responsible directly to the president, thus strengthening him even over his own cabinet ministers, who in the Colombian context of political factionalism and coalitional governments have often shown a real measure of independence.

## The Expansion of the State

The expansion in the capabilities of the state itself has been as impressive as the growth of presidential power over the last several decades, although to distinguish the two is admittedly something of an artificial exercise.

Most striking perhaps has been the development of a wide array of laws and administrative mechanisms to deal with the problems of modern economic and social policy. Thus, the government is now involved in such areas as agrarian reform, public housing, exchange regulation, and the extension of credit to an extent undreamed of a generation ago. The capacity of the central government to carry general policies into effect, and to penetrate effectively the remote geographic and social reaches of the country, has been measurably enhanced as a result.

Meanwhile, such factors as the effective promotion of export diversification, the tightening of economic and other bonds with other Latin American countries (for example, via the Andean Pact), and the augmented capabilities of the government, especially in the economic realm, have somewhat reduced Colombia's external dependence.[40] A good example was President Lleras Restrepo's defiance of the recommendations of the International Monetary Fund concerning devaluation of the peso. In fact, Lleras was able to play so effectively on nationalistic sentiments against the purported dictates of international finance in the matter that for a time he substantially augmented his own domestic popularity.[41]

## Conclusions

In sum, both the Colombian state and Colombian presidents have in recent years increased their power to effect their wills. The result has been to enhance the presidential dominance that has long existed, and to somewhat counteract those rather special factors that made Colombia's president less dominant, nonetheless, than his counterpart in most of Latin America.

To be sure, there have been some countertrends evident. For example, in the 1968 reform Congress was granted more explicit and institutionalized review powers over the economic plans of the government, yet such powers have hardly been utilized. Congress seems little interested in playing such a role and, given its inadequate staffing and access to expertise, is probably incapable of it as well. Nor has Congress made use of a power, granted to it in 1970, to veto executive actions in the area of foreign credit.[42] Talk of the need to decentralize the administrative machinery of the state, and even occasional federalist rumblings from departments or states such as *Antioquia,* have likewise borne little fruit so far.

More important has been the seeming tendency for the army, amid persistent problems of public order that have accentuated its role, to once more assert itself in ways that have potentially important political implications. That President López felt the necessity to purge the army of some of its most able but outspoken officers in May 1975, amid rumors of a possible coup, is a case in point. So far, presidential control of the military appears to remain well in hand, consonant with Colombian tradition and past practice. Yet, the prospects that this relationship might reverse itself in the wake of economic or political crisis, in imitation of so many other erstwhile constitutional regimes in Latin America, should not be entirely discounted. The result would presumably be a crossing of that sometimes tenuous line between presidential dominance and authoritarian rule.

Despite such possibilities, and despite a stronger presidency and a stronger state—all of them consonant with recent trends throughout Latin America—Colombia's president seems unlikely to become a dictator in the immediate future. For he remains circumscribed, though to a lesser extent than formerly, both by the standard political realities of a genuinely constitutional system and, above all, by the historic bonds of the country's elite-directed political factionalism.

## THE CONTEMPORARY PRESIDENCY

It is, finally, necessary to characterize the contemporary Colombian presidency in the light of the impact of these recent trends on its historical configuration.

Each of the five presidents who have held office since the end of military rule in 1958 has confronted a basically similar set of overriding problems and issues, although these have, of course, varied over time in their salience. They include: the preservation of public order in the face of guerrilla violence, kidnappings, and urban disorders; the promotion of economic growth and monetary stability; the assurance of social and political stability through at least some minimal attention to the needs of the mass of the population; and the maintenance of coalition government through the manipulation of the intricate intra- and interparty mechanisms of the National Front and its immediate successor government.

Both in the way policy choices have manifested themselves, and in the ways they have been addressed by the several presidents, with their varied styles and imperatives, the modern Colombian presidency is clearly transitional (or mixed) between what Richard Maullin has called "two different systems of influence and obligation." The first, the traditional or classic, is dominated by the time-honored values and concerns of social status, regionalism, partisan rhetoric, and the formalistic courtesies and romanticism of Hispanic culture. The style of power in the second system is more pragmatic or "industrial," with the stress on instrumental and even scientific solutions to the problems of productivity and social change. As Maullin puts it: "The chief executives of Colombia find that the promotion of a transitional or developing economy resolves itself into the difficult political job of providing leadership for two worlds that are often poorly connected and from time to time in direct conflict."[43] Thus, even a stronger Colombian president, rooted in a state stronger than at any time in the past, must ultimately base much of his ability to accomplish his goals not on his new-found constitutional prerogatives or on the expertise of his technocrats but on his capacity to manage the pressures and manipulate the symbols of the traditional "political country" from which the fundamental constraints on Colombian presidents have always emanated.

## The Presidency of Alberto Lleras Camargo

The problems of public order and of coalition building were necessarily preeminent for Liberal Alberto Lleras Camargo, the first president (1958–62) under the new dispensation of the National Front. Himself a man of compromise, he had served out the last year (1945–46) of Alfonso López Pumarejo's second term and had included Conservatives in his cabinet. Out of the country, notably as secretary-general of the Organization of American States, during much of the period of intense partisan violence during the late 1940s and 1950s, he was in many ways the ideal figure to preside over a coalition government. Even so, economic and social stability could hardly be neglected, and by the end of his administration Colombia had become the first Latin American country to present a formal program of development in accordance with the goals of the Alliance for Progress, and had enacted a significant (though still substantially unimplemented) agrarian reform law. There was little direct pressure from peasants or others for an agrarian reform. Rather, passage of the law required the commitment of the executive and key leaders of the bipartisan coalition, led by Carlos Lleras Restrepo, the Liberal leader in the Senate, who then could cajole and bargain substantially on the basis of considerations of factional interest.[44]

## The Presidency of Guillermo León Valencia

Lleras Camargo's successor, Guillermo León Valencia (1962–66), was a Conservative who in style and manner seemed almost a throwback to the nineteenth century. Valencia was a product of the small southwestern city of Popayán, where traditional values and social patterns continued to predominate. Flowery and somewhat undisciplined in his rhetoric, his appearance added to the impression of a somewhat anachronistic personal style. Yet, Valencia had been one of the early pillars of the National Front, and it was under his administration that the level of violence (2 to 3,000 deaths per year under the Lleras government) was markedly reduced. He even succeeded for a time in uniting the divided Conservative party and including both factions in his government. Although he was regarded generally as a weak president during whose administration little progress was made on economic and social fronts, the overall policies of the previous government were substantially, though less enthusiastically, continued and (apparently under prodding by the United States) tax reforms were enacted in 1963 and 1965.[45] It was also during the Valencia years that the government came to rely more explicitly than ever before on consultations with organized interest groups (apart from party factions) in the formulation of public policy.[46] Less obviously attuned to the "industrial" system of influence and obligation, and above all to its style, than subsequent presidents, the Valencia presidency nonetheless showed unmistakable signs of its advent.

## The Presidency of Carlos Lleras Restrepo

If there is a break in the continuity and style of recent Colombian presidents it occurs here, between the presidency of Valencia and Carlos Lleras Restrepo (1966–70). Lleras Restrepo was the "modern" Colombian president par excellence—not only the architect of the 1961 agrarian reform law, he was also the chief proponent of the constitutional reform of 1968. Himself a pragmatically oriented economist and businessman, he was almost the prototype of a "developmentalist," relying heavily on the emerging group of técnicos to further the ends of his government. His cabinets reflected the trend, relying more heavily on técnicos than politicos, compared to the cabinets of Valencia and Lleras Camargo. At the same time, Lleras reflected the transitional or bifurcated nature of the contemporary Colombian presidency in having deep roots in the Liberal party, having served as its leader or coleader on several occasions. Quintessentially the builder of industrial Colombia, his own career was hardly that of a pure technocrat. Interestingly, in subsequent attempts at a return to the presidency, it seems to have been his failure to attend to the imperatives of the "political country" that has made it unlikely that he will once more have the opportunity to pursue his developmentalist goals.[47]

## The Presidency of Misael Pastrana Borrero

Lleras Restrepo's successor, Misael Pastrana Borrero (1970–74), was a Conservative, in keeping with the principle of presidential alternation. He was very different from President Valencia, however, much more in the industrial than the traditional mold. Indicatively, when the Conservatives in Congress named Evaristo Sourdís, a senator from the Atlantic Coast region, to be the next candidate of the National Front, he was vetoed by the grand old man of conservatism, former president (1946–50) Mariano Ospina Pérez, in favor of a man like Pastrana, who had close ties to the business community of that heartland of Colombian entrepreneurship, the department of Antioquia. The problems of public order and coalition maintenance continued to be important for President Pastrana, but pursuant to the trend initiated under Carlos Lleras the concerns of economic and social policy (including initiatives for an urban reform law) now tended to assume priority.

## The Presidency of Alfonso López Michelsen

Alfonso López Michelsen (1970– ) was the first president to be chosen following the end of alternation. A Liberal, with something of a history as a maverick on the left wing of the party, he received a solid majority of the popular vote and was generally expected to pursue a rather broad reformist program (without, however, really disturbing basic structures). He promptly won from Congress the declaration of an economic emergency and proceeded to decree a more progressive tax structure. Certain features of the economy (export subsidies, for example) were "rationalized," and considerable stimulus was given to the diversification of industrial production. Some of these measures cost López establishment support, while chronic inflation and unemployment led to urban unrest. Resurgent rural violence ("revolutionary" for the past decade, rather than of the traditional interparty variety), kidnappings, a military tinged by corruption and insubordination, and a crackdown on leftists in the universities have further helped to sap much of the initial elan of López' mandato claro. Developmentalist and reformist in orientation, President

López has been plagued both by the inherent strains of the developmental process itself (for example, the tensions between policies designed to promote growth and the more immediate claims of the popular welfare) and the continuing problems of public order and coalition maintenance that remain, even after the formal end of the National Front.

## Conclusions

In sum, policy making for development in a context like the Colombian seems above all to call for strong executive action and planning—action and planning that have become increasingly evident over the last decades. Yet established norms, institutions, and interest groups, and the continuing weaknesses, especially the international vulnerability, of the Colombian state itself, are constraining factors, as are the distinctly living remains of Colombia's traditional system of influence and obligation.

Given such a context, not to mention the social backgrounds and career patterns of the presidents themselves, little in the way of revolutionary change has been forthcoming, nor can it be expected to occur in any near future. To somehow override the traditional patterns of political influence by still further strengthening the presidency might permit the more expeditious promotion of development programs by the president. Yet, to do so—as President Eduardo Frei and the Christian Democrats sought to do during their years in power in Chile—might well serve to weaken the necessary linkages between any constitutional president and the more particularistic concerns of persons and regions, thus in the end depriving the president of an essential degree of popular legitimacy.[48]

Future presidents—though all or most of them will undoubtedly prove to be development-oriented in the wake of Carlos Lleras and his successors—must also remain politicians in the traditional sense. Since they cannot willfully override the concerns of the "political country," let alone the demands of the industrial system of obligation, they will have to reconcile themselves in the foreseeable future, barring unanticipated upheaval, to incremental changes in the pursuit of development goals. The test of any presidentially promoted long-term development policy will thus be the extent to which a series of necessarily short-run tactical actions attuned to the basic requisites of the "political country" can be related to the longer-term goals of "where the country (or a particular president) is going."[49]

Government both in Colombia and throughout Latin American for the foreseeable future will inevitably entail both strong presidents and strong states attuned to the requirements of modern technocracy and the demands of the industrial realm of obligation and influence. To remain or to become once again constitutional, however, they will have to balance such imperatives with the satisfaction of interests of a more parochial and immediate kind—as expressed both by individuals and by groups—which are in the end the stuff of politics for most Colombians, as they are for most people.

## NOTES

1. Jacques Lambert, *Latin America* (Berkeley: University of California Press, 1967).
2. Francisco Leal Buitrago, *Estudio del comportamiento legislativo en Colombia,* vol. 1 (Bogotá: Tercer Mundo, 1973), chap. 4. Congressmen themselves rate ministerial interventions, plus declarations of urgency and similar means of communication, as the two principal means of influence of the executive on Congress. See Harvey F. Kline, "Orientación hacia el Ejecutivo," in Gary Hoskin et al., *Estudio del comportamiento legislativo en Colombia,* vol. 2 (Bogotá: Tercer Mundo, 1975), p. 361.
3. For the long Colombian tradition of "extraordinary" powers and discretionary decree-powers, see David Bushnell, *The Santander Regime in Gran Colombia* (Newark: University of Delaware Press, 1954), pp. 31–34.
4. Quoted in Armando Borrero, "El Proceso Legislativo," in Hoskin et al., op. cit., p. 123.
5. Reid Reading, "Early Socialization to Impersonal Political Institutions: Some United States-Latin American Comparisons" (unpublished manuscript). This is not to say that the president is necessarily regarded as a benevolent figure, however; cf. Reading, "Political Socialization in Colombia and the United States: An Exploratory Study," *Midwest Journal of Political Science* 12 (1968): 352–81.
6. James L. Payne, *Patterns of Conflict in Colombia* (New Haven: Yale University Press, 1968), chap. 11.
7. See the discussion in Robert H. Dix, *Colombia: The Political Dimensions of Change* (New Haven: Yale University Press, 1967), pp. 179–84; see also Payne, op. cit., chap. 3.
8. For the regionalist basis of congressional resistance to the president, see Gary Hoskin, "Dimensions of Representation in the Colombian National Legislature," in Weston Agor, ed., *Latin American Legislatures: Their Role and Influence* (New York: Praeger, 1971), p. 437.
9. Quoted in Richard Maullin, *The Colombia-IMF Disagreement of November-December 1966: An Interpretation of its Place in Colombian Politics.* RAND Corporation Memorandum RM-5314-RC (Santa Monica, Calif.: RAND, 1967), p. 10.
10. Kline, op. cit., p. 363.
11. Richard Bird argues that both the 1953 tax reform and the enactment of the 1965 sales tax are indicative of the relative independence of government decision makers from the importunities of interest groups, at least in the industrial sector, provided the government is strong and determined. He assesses the power of interest groups in the agricultural sector to be greater, however: Richard M. Bird, *Taxation and Development: Lessons from the Colombian Experience* (Cambridge, Mass.: Harvard University Press, 1970), p. 197.
12. Mauricio Solaún, Fernando Cepeda, and Bruce Bagley, "Urban Reform in Colombia: The Impact of the 'Politics of Games' on Public Policy," in Francine Rabinovitz and Felicity M. Trueblood, eds. *Latin American Urban Research,* vol. 3 (Beverly Hills: Sage Publications, 1973), p. 113.
13. Harvey F. Kline, "Grupos de presión en el Congreso colombiano," in Hoskin et al., op. cit., pp. 334–37.
14. See Albert O. Hirschman, *Journeys Toward Progress* (New York: Twentieth Century Fund, 1963), esp. chap. 3.
15. The Church's vacillation between two Conservative candidates was a contributing factor in the Liberal victory in 1930. An account of this episode may be found in Guillermo Salamanca, *La republica liberal,* vol. 1 (Bogotá: Editorial "El Voto Nacional," 1961).
16. Solaún et al., op. cit. For a good discussion of the constraints of public opinion on Colombia's foreign exchange policy, see Richard R. Nelson, T. Paul Schultz, and Robert L.

Slighton, *Structural Change in a Developing Economy* (Princeton: Princeton University Press, 1971), chap. 7.

17. Ernest Duff assesses the extractive capability (that is, the ability to collect taxes) of the Colombian government and its regulative capability as being quite low in comparison to other Latin American nations. See his "The Role of Congress in the Colombian Political System," in Agor, op. cit., p. 375. Nelson et al., op. cit., p. 305, point up the constraints on development policy of the Colombian government's limited administrative resources.

18. Ibid., pp. 238–39. The authors warn, however, "that it is difficult to use such incidents to support the hypothesis that international lending authorities have substantial 'leverage' in inducing a country to make policy changes it would not undertake in the absence of external pressures," (pp. 239–40). Domestic considerations were present as well. For a portrayal of the dependence of the Colombian budget on foreign trade, see Bird, op. cit., pp. 35–36.

19. The longest regime in Colombian history, that of Rafael Núñez, a civilian, lasted ten years (1884–94); he also held the presidency earlier, from 1880–82. Mosquera held power on three occasions for a total of eight years. The twentieth-century president with the longest tenure has been Alfonso López Pumarejo (1934–38 and 1942–45).

20. The constitution of 1863, which remained in force until 1885, divided Colombia into states and declared them to be sovereign, dubbing the country the United States of Colombia. The constitution of 1858 had previously established a less extreme version of a federal regime.

21. See Payne, op. cit., pp. 281–84.

22. Again, exceptions would include Costa Rica and pre-1973 Chile. Some of these limits, however, at least in the Colombian case, have proved to be more formal than real.

23. For a fuller discussion of the origins and nature of the National Front, see Dix, op. cit., chap. 6.

24. The coleqiado was a nine-member plural executive that governed Uruguay from 1952 to 1966. According to the constitution six members were to represent the majority party and three the minority. A modified version of the coleqiado had existed between 1919 and 1934, as well.

25. Jockey Club, Bogotá, *Informe a la Asamblea General de Socios* (1964). The exception, President Guillermo León Valencia, was the scion of a notable family from the southwestern city of Popayán and the son of a former president. Others among the losing presidential candidates during this period were also members of the Jockey Club.

26. For an account of early efforts to do so, see Bushnell, op. cit., chap. 16.

27. Colombia has been one of the few countries in Latin America with several regions of relatively balanced economic strength and population, each with a major urban center. Cf. Dix, op. cit., pp. 21–23.

28. The alternative model was that of the unifying autocracy. Gino Germani, *Política y sociedad en una epoca de transición de la sociedad tradicional a la sociedad de masas* (Buenos Aires: Paidos, 1962), chap. 6. The fact that much of the army that liberated Colombia was Venezuelan in origin may have contributed to the initial suspicion of the army on the part of civilian elites, as well as giving the military an initially lower salience and status in Colombian society. The first coup and dictatorship in the country's history (1830) were carried out by a Venezuelan (General Rafael Urdaneta).

29. Cf. Duff, op. cit., p. 391. See also Payne, op. cit., esp. chap. 10, for an elaboration of these points.

30. See Dix, op. cit., pp. 82–91, for details concerning López' so-called *revolución en marcha*. For an essentially Marxist interpretation of these developments, see Leal Buitrago, op. cit., pp. 33–54.

31. Cf. the comment in Hoskin, "Dimensions of Representation," op. cit., pp. 416–17, and the discussion in Borrero, op. cit. Alfonso López Michelsen, then head of a dissident Liberal faction that had just rejoined the main body of the party under his instigation, commented that his support of the constitutional reform was a "*puente de plata*" for the reunification of the Liberal

party: quoted in Jaime Vidal Perdomo, *Historia de la reforma constitucional de 1968 y sus alcances jurídicos* (Bogotá: Universidad Externado de Colombia, 1970), p. 75. The provisions of the reform and the arguments concerning them may be found in this volume.

32. Gary Hoskin, "El congreso colombiano: Paraíso del país político, sombra del modelo formal," in Hoskin et al., op. cit., p. 374.

33. Article 122 permits the executive to declare a state of emergency for a period of 90 days. During this time he may issue decrees with the force of law on the specifically declared subject of the emergency (such as the economy). Congress must be convoked if it is not in session and may repeal the presidential decrees, although this seems unlikely to happen in practice.

34. The difficulty—and therefore one of the effective limits imposed by Article 122—lay at least in part with the fact that there was no clear state of economic crisis: cf. Solaún et al., op. cit., n. 29, p. 128.

35. For the opinions of congressmen to this effect, see Kline, "Orientación hacia el ejecutivo," op. cit., pp. 358–59.

36. For a discussion of this point, see Vidal Perdomo, op. cit., pp. 161–62.

37. This is not to say that there is no overlap between the directors of interest groups and ministerial incumbency, however. Cf. Pablo Hernan Gómez, *Concentración del poder económico en Colombia* (Bogotá: Centro de Investigación y Acción Social, 1974), pp. 50–51.

38. Andrés Moreno, "The Effect of Organizational Structure on the Effectiveness of Interest Groups: The Case of Colombia" (Ph.D. dissertation, Rice University, 1976), chap. 4.

39. Under the circumstances the president failed to push the matter and it died in Congress; Solaún et al., op. cit., p. 113.

40. Between 1962 and 1974, Colombia was able to progressively reduce its dependence on coffee exports by half, from 84 percent of the total value of exports to 42 percent. Data are from the Colombian *Departmento Administrativo Nacional de Estadística* (DANE) and the *Instituto Colombiano de Comercio Exterior* (INCOMEX) as cited in Colombia, *Directorio de exportadores,* 1975 (Bogotá: Banco de la República, 1975), p. 62.

41. Maullin, op. cit.

42. Hoskin, "El congreso colombiano," in Hoskin et al., op. cit., pp. 384–85.

43. Maullin, op. cit., p. 3.

44. The background and legislative progress of the 1961 agrarian reform law are well elaborated in Hirschman, op. cit., chap. 3. Alberto Lleras Camargo and Carlos Lleras Restrepo are cousins and both are Liberals, but they have not been particularly close politically.

45. Dix, op. cit., p. 409n.

46. This was symptomatic of the fact that reliance on the traditional "political country," although crucial, was not sufficient for the solution of the problems of the modern presidency.

47. To wit, Lleras' faction received only 19 percent of the total Liberal vote in the midterm elections of 1976.

48. President Frei's approach to the presidency, and in particular the "Gaullist" constitutional reforms of 1969 that considerably strengthened the president vis-a-vis Congress, tended to have this effect, according to Arturo Valenzuela and Alexander Wilde, "Presidential Politics and the Decline of the Chilean Congress," in Lloyd Musolf and Joel Smith, eds., *Legislatures and Political Development* (Durham, N.C.: Duke University Press, 1976).

49. Cf. Bird, op. cit., p. 305, and chap. 6 generally.

CHAPTER

# 6

## THE VENEZUELAN
## PRESIDENTIAL SYSTEM
### John D. Martz

In an interpretive study of Venezuelan constitutionalism, its current minister of foreign relations, Ramón Escovar Salom, once wrote: "Presidentialism
has been the center of gravity in our political organization. Historically it has
been traditional for the President to succeed himself, by means of a constitutional reform which permits his reelection or the imposition of a chosen
successor." As Zum Felde had written of Uruguay, he added, the patterns of
Venezuelan constitutionalism customarily generated exaggerated presidentialism, and from this came turmoil and upheaval. The constitution of 1961, which
retained the broad scope of executive powers, was viewed as consistent with
the national heritage and necessary for solidification of the post-1958 system
of reformist democracy.[1]

History bears indisputable witness to the dominant role of the national
*caudillo,* whether civil or military. From the first moment of independence in
1830, Venezuelan political leadership has been marked by a strongly personalist exercise of power and authority. During the nineteenth century this was not
functional for national politics, with chronic instability the dominant theme.
As one president wryly noted, "The country is like a dry hide; you step on it
on one end and it pops up on the other."[2] Even more importantly, the social
and economic structure endured throughout the century without marked
change, notwithstanding such scattered events as the abolition of slavery in
1854 and shifting periods of regional hegemony in public affairs. By the close
of the 1800s, Venezuela remained dependent upon a one-product economy
(coffee); education was the preserve of a small elite; cultural influences
were narrowly circumscribed by the caudillo of the moment; and the armed
forces were merely factional bands lacking in military training and profes-
sionalism.[3]

This was to change in 1908 with the accession to power of General Juan Vicente Gómez, the "Tyrant of the Andes."[4] During the 27 years that followed, a concentration of power was achieved for the first time. The result was a shift in political, moral, and economic patterns. Gómez shrewdly and efficiently centralized presidential power, mightily assisted by the new income generated by petroleum wealth. Notwithstanding certain virtues in the revisionist views of some contemporary scholars toward Gómez, it was also true, in the words of conservative historian Guillermo Morón, that his period "produced social loosening and moral deformation in the generations who had to live it through. The ideas of political liberty and civic integrity lacked all meaning since public feeling was blunted. Any voice which made a criticism was silenced; the gaol or exile was Gómez' 'peace.' "[5]

The intellectual rationale for the dictatorship was by no means inconsistent with the heritage of presidential caudillism. Laureano Vallenilla Lanz, Gómez' resident theoretician, expounded at length in his *Cesarismo democrático.*[6] The sociological composition of Venezuela was described as requiring a "necessary policeman" to harmonize and defend national unity. The establishment and maintenance of order, given the existing stage of national evolution, could only be realized through the "democratic Caesar." Thus, Vallenilla provided not only an apologia for the regime, but extended advocacy of the centrality of presidential authority. As such, it stood as a logical outgrowth of Venezuelan historical experience. Yet, the 40 years that followed the 1935 death of Gómez have been marked by major political transformation, nowhere so pronounced as in the expansion and institutionalization of political participation.

The clarion call for systemic democratization had already been trumpeted earlier by the uprising of the "Generation of '28"[7]; organizational bases were laid and popular attitudes altered from 1935–48.[8] With the reestablishment of democratic government following the decade of *perezjimenista* dictatorship and repression, Venezuelan political elites built a highly competitive, party-based system that stands today as the most vigorous in Latin America.[9] At the same time, the power and authority of presidentialism are hallmarks of contemporary Venezuelan politics. As with any political system, both formal and informal characteristics abound. That is, an understanding of legal and constitutional powers must be complemented by consideration of political dynamics.

Venezuelan presidentialism today is strongly influenced by nonconstitutional elements that impinge in a variety of ways upon the exercise of power. On the one hand, such functions as that of the party leadership substantially strengthen presidential authority. Yet, there are concomitant constraints that limit the scope of the executive. These realities of the political system are, if unwritten, sufficiently germane to merit consideration. Furthermore, the experience of four different presidents since 1958 speaks to the importance of personal leadership, and will also be examined. Ultimately, we will conclude that contemporary Venezuelan politics is appropriately characterized as presidential, with a perceptible infusion of civilian caudillism reflecting the national heritage, but that at the same time there are a host of factors providing sharp constraints upon the exercise of power.

## CONSTITUTIONAL PARAMETERS OF PRESIDENTIAL POWER

The constitution of 1961 establishes certain requisites for presidential eligibility (Articles 182–85). These include Venezuelan citizenship by birth, an age of more than 30, and secular status. Election goes to the candidate receiving a relative majority of votes, chosen by universal direct suffrage. From the day of nomination until election, the candidate may not serve as a minister, state governor, or secretary to the presidency. A former president is denied eligibility for reelection until ten years have passed since his previous incumbency. Thus, Rómulo Betancourt (1959–64) only became eligible for another term in the 1973 elections. Similarly, Rafael Caldera (1969–74) cannot be a candidate in 1978, but could run in 1983. In addition, a 1973 constitutional amendment—designed to prohibit the candidacy of former dictator Marcos Pérez Jiménez—disqualified any public official who had been tried and found guilty of misconduct during earlier service at the higher levels of national government.

Presidential powers are broad and explicit. They may be catalogued under three different rubrics: actions independent of nonexecutive authority; actions requiring cabinet approval; and measures subject to congressional review and approval.

### Independent Authority

The range of independent authority includes the right to name and to replace cabinet ministers, state governors, and high-ranking functionaries in many of the independent agencies that by law report directly to the president. He is also empowered to manage foreign affairs and enter into international agreements, to administer national finances, to grant pardons, and to exercise his role as commander in chief of the armed forces, including the specific authority to fix its size. Among the forms of decree power—some of which require congressional authorization—the president may himself create state-affiliated autonomous agencies. As the Venezuelan state progressively enlarges its areas of direct responsibility, a host of such entities has come into being. A few of the more important are the *Corporación Venezolana de Fomento*

(CVF), *Instituto Nacional de Obras Sanitarias* (INOS), *Instituto Agrario Nacional* (IAN), and *Corporación Venezolana de Guayana* (CVG).

## Cabinet-Approved Powers

Powers requiring cabinet or congressional approval are so designed as a method of curbing executive abuses. While this has been meaningful with Congress, it is clearly less effective in cases in which the cabinet must be consulted. Prior to 1961, for example, the president was required to secure the consent of his ministers before abolishing or altering public services. In practice the restriction was ineffective; such measures must now pass the Congress as well. The present constitution nonetheless grants extensive decree powers that are subject only to the approval of the cabinet. Among the more notable are the declaration of a state of emergency, partially or totally suspending constitutional guarantees for as long as 90 days (although Congress must be consulted within ten days); adoption of measures to defend the republic and its sovereignty in time of international crisis; the issuing of extraordinary economic or financial measures; and the convocation of special congressional sessions.

These attributes are incorporated into Article 190, with the requirement of cabinet approval set forth in its final sections. Presidential power of appointment and removal of cabinet members obviously vitiates any likelihood of effective rebellion against the president once he has decided an issue. At the same time, the collective discussion and ultimate judgment of the cabinet may well influence him. In a technical sense there are actually two executive organs —the council of ministers and the cabinet. The former term applies to the meetings of ministers convened and chaired by the president, with collective decisions reached by a two-thirds vote. In addition to the administrative heads of the ministries, the governor of the Federal District is also present and exercises voice and vote on issues concerning his jurisdiction. Decisions reached by the council of ministers are treated as both the joint and individual responsibility of all those in attendance, unless a negative vote was cast.

While the executive branch has traditionally numbered 13 ministers, President Pérez created several new ministries and restructured others in 1976. Moreover, there has been a trend toward the extension of ministerial rank to officials outside the customary structure, for example, the minister for international economic affairs. (This has been especially pronounced under Pérez.) Such individuals, frequently among the most influential members of the administration, may also attend meetings of the council of ministers. Upon invitation, such other officials as presidents of autonomous state agencies may also participate. Predictably the collective strength of the council will vary, reflecting both the personality and style of the president. Should the council include prominent political independents, as is often the case, its voice may receive particular attention. When the administration is a multiparty coalition, additional political elements also heighten the probability of presidential responsiveness to the council.

## Congressional Review and Approval

Nonetheless, congressional restraints upon executive authority understandably constitute a more important legal safeguard against arbitrary acts by a president. These largely follow patterns familiar to students of Western constitutions. The usual array of policy-making areas is enumerated as the responsibility of either the upper or lower chamber, or in some cases both. Legislation may be introduced from the executive: the most usual pattern is presentation of proposed legislation by a representative of the president's political party on the floor of Congress. In any event, passage by majority vote leads to consideration by the president. He must act within ten days, wither signing the measure into law or returning it to the legislature for further action. In the latter case, he may ask for modification of specified portions of the bill or request its complete reconsideration.

Sitting in joint session, the legislators attempt to deal with presidential objections, the results of which are sent back to him. If the bill is approved by two-thirds of those present and voting, the president is required to promulgate it unchanged within five days. Should the vote be by simple majority, however, he has the option of returning it within five days for final reconsideration. At that point congressional action by simple majority also requires presidential approval within five days.

A variation of this arises if the president grounds his objections on constitutional issues. Thus, he has the option of soliciting a decision from the Supreme Court of Justice as to a bill's alleged unconstitutionality. The court must decide the issue within ten days. If the president is upheld, the legislation becomes a dead letter. Should the justices deny the existence of unconstitutional provisions, however, the bill must then be promulgated within five days of that decision.

As with many constitutional systems, authority over the power of the purse constitutes a major point of friction between the two branches of national government. Budget proposals by the administration require congressional approval, and its practical role has grown sharply in recent years. Congress has been substantially aided by the office of the comptroller general, which is authorized to supervise and audit national accounts, revenues, and expenditures. The comptroller general himself, customarily a political independent, is chosen by joint session of Congress within 30 days of each new constitutional term. He prepares and submits annual reports to the legislature on the fiscal performance of government agencies, a responsibility that in practice is taken quite seriously. Congress thus benefits from this source of detailed information on the administrative and fiscal management of executive offices.

An important legislative organ is the Delegated Commission, a form of minicongress that functions during the six months when Congress is in recess. Composed of the presiding officers of the Senate and Chamber of Deputies, along with 21 other members of Congress, its representation is proportionate to the partisan make-up of Congress. Empowered to convene a special session of Congress if it chooses, the Delegated Commission exercises substantial limitations upon presidential authority. Its approval is required for executive decrees of expenditures not previously authorized in the budget. The president may not modify or abolish public organs and agencies without the agreement of the commission. Its constitutional role is important, then, and may well constitute a brake upon presidential initiative.

There are several other constitutional provisions by which the Congress limits presidential power. For one, it may vote a motion of censure against a cabinet minister—if the motion passes by a two-thirds vote, the president is required to replace the minister. There are also restrictions upon supplemental budgetary decrees. Before 1961, the president had been empowered to allocate additional funds to the national budget after its original approval by Congress. The Special Reserve Fund, created through cash surpluses in the treasury, had provided a source from which the president could unilaterally decree new expenditures. For many years this led to increases of from 20 to 40 percent over the original budget, a practice that reached its apogee under Pérez Jiménez. In response to such abuses, the present constitution specifies that any such measure requires prior approval of Congress or the Delegated Commission.

There are also restrictions on presidential travel, whereby he may not leave national territory without congressional approval. Although generally regarded as having only symbolic value, this common feature of Latin American constitutions is not necessarily ineffectual, as Chile's Eduardo Frei learned in 1967. Frequent trips since 1959 by Venezuelan presidents, to be sure, have never been denied. When leaving the country, the president designates one of his ministers as acting president—in practice, the minister of interior relations has been tapped. Congress has no role in the choice although, if the president is absent more than 90 consecutive days, the legislators in joint session may strip him of office.

## POLITICAL REALITIES OF PRESIDENTIAL POWER

Although constitutional provisions and legal regulation help to define and circumscribe political behavior, important variables lie beyond such written norms. The exercise of presidential power in post-1958 Venezuela has been marked by several informal sources of both authority and constraint. The major ones fall into distinct, if interrelated, categories: the configuration of the party system and composition of the administration; the politics of interest groups; and the context of prevailing public opinion. The role of presidential leadership style is also crucial—to such a degree that it will be considered separately later in this chapter.

## The Multiparty System

The characteristic multiparty basis of contemporary Venezuelan politics serves both to enhance and to limit presidential authority. The proliferation of new parties, along with the fragmentation of several older ones, was a marked trend until 1973, when the two parties of an emergent political establishment, *Acción Democrática* (AD) and the Social Christian *Comité de Organización Política Electoral Independiente* (COPEI), together polled 85 percent of the vote for their respective presidential candidates. As a consequence, presidents have often found themselves confronted by a hostile majority in Congress. The necessity for compromise and conciliation has become a major theme of Venezuelan government,[10] thereby erecting barriers to the exercise of executive authority. In addition, Venezuelan presidents have frequently found themselves heading a multiparty coalition. Bargaining with the leadership of other member parties of government has become a familiar characteristic of the political panorama.

In 1959 Rómulo Betancourt entered the presidency at the head of a coalition including his own Acción Democrática, COPEI, and the *Unión Republicana Democrática* (URD). Committed to a multiparty government of national conciliation in the wake of the perezjimenista decade, he began with the participation of all national parties less the *Partido Comunista de Venezuela* (PCV), which was intentionally excluded. Despite the subsequent withdrawal of the URD following policy differences over the handling of the Cuban question, Betancourt's AD-COPEI coalition, the famous *guanabana,** initially retained a congressional majority. COPEI played a crucially important role in the survival of Venezuelan democracy under Betancourt, at a time when the president was confronted with urban terrorism from the revolutionary left, abortive rightist military uprisings, an assassination attempt engineered by the Dominican dictator Rafael Leonidas Trujillo, and economic woes as a final legacy of the 1948–58 dictatorship.

Betancourt's freedom of action was understandably affected by the participation of COPEI, for it was necessary to secure agreement from leaders of

---

*Now a familiar term in the Venezuelan political lexicon, this referred to the guanabana fruit —green (COPEI) on the outside and white (AD) inside.

both parties on many policy issues. Occasional differences of party outlook and ambition also were expressed. By way of illustration, the agrarian reform program—a cornerstone of administration policy—was subjected to the inevitable complications resulting from *copeyano* leadership of the agriculture ministry and *adeco* control of the National Agrarian Institute. Circumstances grew even more difficult as the result of two divisions within Betancourt's own party: the departure of its left wing in 1960 on ideological grounds, and that of the *arsista* faction (a faction whose acronym ARS referred to a leading Venezuelan advertising agency) two years later, following an internal struggle for control of the party machinery. The second of these left the AD-COPEI coalition without a congressional majority, and only with difficulty could Betancourt secure legislative cooperation in the final months of his administration.

Coalition government remained during much of the next term, although its composition was different. The multiplication of political parties had produced seven presidential contenders in 1963, and the victorious Raúl Leoni of Acción Democrática received but one-third of the vote. Despite the wishes of the outgoing Betancourt, the guanabana was not extended. Instead, Leoni painstakingly put together a heterogeneous alliance with the URD and the *Frente Nacional Democrático* (FND). Known as the *Ancha Base* (Broad Base), it combined similar reformist orientations of the AD and URD with the business-oriented FND, at best an awkward combination. The FND withdrew after some 16 months, while the URD remained until late in the term, when it left to mount its separate 1968 electoral campaign.

Presidential authority was consequently more limited under Leoni than under Betancourt. COPEI's stance of "autonomy of action" meant that its support was sometimes available to the administration, thus broadening Leoni's options, but also requiring yet greater political bargaining and conciliation. By 1968, with some two dozen organizations competing either nationally or regionally—and with Acción Democrática having undergone yet another schism—the need for congressional alliances appeared greater than ever. When Social Christian leader Rafael Caldera won the presidency with 29 percent of the vote, it was expected that another multiparty government would be formed. Instead, Caldera chose not to constitute a coalition, and from 1969–74 Venezuela enjoyed a one-party administration.

Presidential power was, therefore, further subjected to the constraints of Venezuela's multiparty condition. Caldera, whose personal stature and authority were substantial, successfully played the role of a strong chief executive. At the same time, his party's minority status made it impossible to fulfill some of his policies. Although a number of important policies were adopted during Caldera's administration, those requiring legislative approval were necessarily subjected to the views and pressures of opposition political parties. Shifting congressional alliances and ad hoc coalitions had to be negotiated—

as, for example, with the Hydrocarbons Reversion Law of 1971.[11] Thus, the Congress was of continual importance and provided a constant check on the exercise of executive authority.

With the 1973 election of the AD's Carlos Andrés Pérez, the situation shifted dramatically. Pérez enjoyed the luxury of an outright majority in both houses of Congress, thus party alliances at either the ministerial or legislative level were unnecessary. More than any other post-1958 president, Pérez was in a position to provide uncommonly strong political leadership. On some important issues he has made a concerted effort to win the approval of the opposition. The most striking case has been the quest for broad nonpartisan approval of oil nationalization, discussed later in this chapter.[12]

The experience of the four presidents since 1958, then, has included both coalition and single-party administrations. Without exception, however, the circumstantial configuration of the national party system and the composition of the government have provided very real constraints upon the incumbent presidents.

## The Influence of Interest Groups

A second factor to influence and impinge upon the political realities of presidential power is that of interest groups. Four can be cited for illustrative purposes: organized labor, the peasantry, the private sector, and the military. Pressures from the first have come largely from the *Confederación de Trabajadores de Venezuela* (CTV). Formally created in November 1947,[13] it was organized and directed for many years by leaders of Acción Democrática. This obviously provided support to AD governments. During the Betancourt years the CTV largely subordinated immediate labor-related goals to the broader objective of strengthening democratic government in Venezuela. Labor-management conflict was minimized, while the CTV repeatedly threw its organizational and symbolic strength behind Betancourt to help ensure survival of the regime in the face of major challenges from both left and right.

The labor movement has continued to exert powerful pressure on national politics. A sharp manifestation was its decisive support of the Leoni presidential nomination. In a sense repaying Leoni for his sympathetic treatment while minister of labor from 1945–48, the labor wing of AD was instrumental in securing his victory at the party convention. It continued to provide important backing throughout the Leoni administration, although this has been somewhat reduced since the 1967 division of Acción Democrática. Badly divided by that internecine struggle, the CTV found many of its leaders—including its president, José González Navarro—siding with Luis B. Prieto and his *Movimiento Electoral del Pueblo* (MEP). Since 1967 Venezuelan labor has consequently been far less monolithic. CTV leadership itself is shared by members of COPEI, MEP, and the AD, while some individual unions have adopted a more leftist posture and stand outside the CTV. Yet, the interests of labor continue to constitute an important factor in politics, and today are being articulated with increasing authority, given the progressive diminution of the MEP and the AD return to power.

Related to the CTV is its peasant affiliate, the *Federación Campesina de Venezuela* (FCV).[14] Similarly built and organized by AD leaders, its political leanings were especially important for the Betancourt government. Indeed, the effort by the revolutionary left to mount an insurgency of the *fidelista* model was thwarted in part because of campesino loyalties to Betancourt, Acción Democrática, and the elected regime. Betancourt's own stature was especially germane, for from his early years in politics particular emphasis had been devoted to the rural population. When he won the 1958 elections with a preponderance of rural support, Betancourt was most likely the most familiar and admired political leader with the peasantry. He effectively cultivated and maintained support through frequent weekend trips to the interior, personally delivering deeds for land in the implementation of the agrarian reform program.

The influence of Venezuela's economic elites has been important in the contemporary political system. Its most public and powerful manifestation is *Fedecámaras*—the Federation of Chambers of Industry and Commerce. With representatives from all branches of private business, it exerts pressure on relevant government policy, sometimes with considerable effect. Its opposition to Venezuelan entry into the Andean Pact, for instance, delayed the nation's joining for several years. Raúl Leoni was unable to negotiate such entry, which was only achieved by the Caldera government. Even so, Fedecámaras has continued to take sharp issue with many aspects of its implementation. This produced limitations on the Caldera administration's freedom of action, as has been the case more recently with Pérez. Although Fedecámaras is but one of several voices with which the private sector speaks, its impact on national policy making is illustrative of yet another constraint upon executive action.

A fourth major group is the armed forces. While its corporate commitment to political democracy and civilian leadership has steadily increased since 1958, the military remains an important power contender, to use Anderson's phrase.[15] Each president has devoted major time and attention to his relationship with the armed forces, assiduously seeking their support, asking counsel on many issues, and consulting them with meticulous care. The sheer survival of the Betancourt administration despite an extraordinary array of antagonistic forces provided testimony to his exceptional political acumen. If Betancourt travelled to the interior frequently to meet with peasants and to distribute titles of ownership to the previously landless, he pointedly visited local military headquarters, lodging and eating at the barracks. Both Leoni and Caldera also maintained personal and institutional ties with the military, as has Pérez.

Pérez, for example, toured the nation shortly after his 1973 election as a means of thanking the electorate for its support. An important detail in his itinerary was a large number of personal visits to military headquarters in the towns where he was appearing. His attention to the armed forces was also exemplified by personal consultation with the officer corps during the months required for passage of oil nationalization in 1975. In the process, his painstaking explanations of the proposed legislation to the military were in some ways as important as those with members of opposition political parties. In short, presidential attention to the military goes far beyond discussion of questions specifically tied to the armed forces as institutions. Such current issues as boundary negotiations with Colombia and Guyana and colonization programs in areas contiguous to the Brazilian border are but a few of the policy areas about which the executive is clearly dependent upon a modicum of support and sympathy from the Venezuelan military.

## The Impact of Public Opinion

The exercise of presidential authority, then, must take into account the interests and influence of the preceding as well as other groups within the polity. Given the competitive electoral base of the contemporary system, such elements are fundamental to the president. Similarly, Venezuela is a nation in which the impact of public opinion must be reckoned with. While a more amorphous and less readily defined political force than those mentioned above, public opinion constitutes a factor that any president must continuously recognize. Providing a potential source for the enunciation of leadership, it also possesses the ability indirectly to insist upon standards and norms of presidential behavior.

In electoral terms, public opinion will exert particular pressure on government policy during a national campaign; to put it more precisely, an administration during an electoral campaign will attempt to respond to immediate needs and demands. Setting aside the partisan charges of *ventajismo* (personal gain or advantage) with which each incumbent government is attacked during the competition for succession, it remains true that fundamental bread-and-butter issues affecting the broad public will elicit especially careful attention. Whatever the responses of the administration, it is not insensitive to public opinion when the forthcoming electoral verdict may hang in the balance. Presidential affiliation with his own party inevitably shapes his actions during the campaign months to some extent, however.

In 1963, President Betancourt was primarily concerned with the survival and strengthening of the democratic system, and many of his actions—necessarily shaped by the urban violence of the *Fuerzas Armadas de Liberación Nacional* (FALN)—also spoke directly to the public, to its need of physical security and desire for a peaceful political succession. Five years later Raúl

Leoni saw the putative hegemony of his party threatened by its third division, and was influenced by the need to solidify Acción Democrática against the challenge of its former colleagues in the MEP. At the same time, it was necessary to prepare the way for a smooth transition to the opposition should COPEI win, which it eventually did. And in 1973, rising inflation and periodic shortages of basic food staples—in considerable part the outgrowth of international pressures beyond the full control of the Caldera government—contributed to a public lack of enthusiasm over the copeyano nominee, Lorenzo Fernández. Indeed, a nationwide survey of public opinion conducted by Enrique A. Baloyra and the author clearly demonstrated the primacy of economic issues in the formation of electoral preferences by the Venezuelan voters.[16]

Public opinion also impinges upon presidential authority at times other than during electoral campaigns, and may be subject to organization on behalf of certain policy positions. Such was the "Association of the Middle Class" organized by Guillermo Morón in 1966. Constituted to oppose the Leoni government's proposed income tax reforms, it joined with opposition parties and the business community, eventually forcing major concessions from the president.

Often it is a broader and more generalized concern that is reflected by public opinion. Such contemporary questions as those of foreign policy toward Cuba and nationalization of oil are illustrative. Public dismay over the depth of administrative inefficiency and outright corruption in the bureaucracy have produced an increasing stream of public denunciations from all quarters. Former president Betancourt has repeatedly expressed deep concern, while on January 2, 1976 Carlos Andrés Pérez candidly declared that the nation's public service had become seriously corrupt.

Entirely aside from formal constitutional provisions, then, the president is subject to a variety of informal constraints emanating from prevailing political circumstances and from many institutional and associational forces. Although these have been treated largely as limiting his scope of action, the converse may also occur. An electoral mandate such as that of Pérez, for instance, provided him with initial freedom greater than that of his three predecessors. The support of selected interest groups may also enhance executive authority. The extent to which the president truly controls his own political party is also relevant, as is the organization's strength. Beyond such factors, moreover, lies the variable of presidential leadership style.

## STYLES OF PRESIDENTIAL LEADERSHIP

None of Venezuela's elected chief executives has, by any stretch of the imagination, been a weak president. Certainly the tradition of forceful national leadership has remained basic in Venezuelan government. Yet, each has demonstrated his own idiosyncratic presidential style, even aside from the particular political realities that marked his term of office. Brief examination of selected policy decisions helps to depict the respective approaches of Betancourt, Leoni, Caldera, and Pérez. Those pertaining to foreign policy show themselves less subject to constraints than those of a domestic nature. Taken together, however, they sketch a collage that offers a broader perspective on contemporary patterns of presidential power in Venezuela.

## The Presidency of Rómulo Betancourt (1959–64)

For Rómulo Betancourt, in 1959 the first elected president following the decade of military rule, a basic task was promoting the fullest possible understanding, and strengthening of, democratic principles. This came under sharp and continuous attack from both the reactionary right and from leftist revolutionaries. During much of his administration, questions of democracy and civil liberties received high priority. His handling of such critical issues, although far too complex to be discussed at length, was suggestive of both the constitutional and informal exercise of presidential power.[17] This was starkly outlined during the final months of 1963, as the presidential campaign moved toward its climax in the face of the FALN pledge to disrupt and block what it termed an imperialist farce dictated from Washington.

Despite periodic selective suspensions of constitutional rights, the effort to maintain civil liberties had been foremost in the government's thinking. Congress continued to function normally, among other things providing a useful platform from which the left attacked Betancourt under the umbrella of congressional immunity. Until September 1963 only three congressmen had been subjected to executive action: two communist members were jailed following the lifting of parliamentary immunity by the Chamber of Deputies and after evidence of their involvement in insurrectional activities was received; the third, a deputy from the *Movimiento de la Izquierda Revolucionaria* (MIR), had remained at liberty when the chamber refused the executive request for the lifting of immunity.

The terrorist campaign intensified in August and September of that year, climaxed by armed attack on an excursion train between Los Teques and El Encanto which resulted in the death of five national guardsmen and the wounding of several civilians. Great public wrath was provoked, and Betancourt ordered the immediate arrest of communist and *mirista* congressmen, notwithstanding congressional immunity. The action was justified by Article 143 of the constitution, which permitted a 96-hour house arrest of congressmen in the event of flagrant abuses of immunity. At the conclusion of this period they were turned over to military courts on the grounds that such jurisdiction was justified by alleged crimes against the constitution. Some argued that the constitutional grounds were specious and the action illegal. For Betancourt, however, the nature of terrorist attacks, as well as the state of public opinion, made the arrests both necessary and politically feasible. Significantly, there was virtually no opposition from nongovernment democratic parties, despite the approach of elections, and the campaign continued in a highly partisan and argumentative fashion. With Leoni's victory, Venezuela in March 1964 experienced its first peaceful transition from one democratically elected president to another.

One highly sympathetic scholar, Robert J. Alexander, has written that such suspension of constitutional guarantees "was a partial defeat." As Betancourt himself had reiterated, the regime was pledged to carry out a social revolution in a democratic manner. Thus, in Alexander's view, "restriction on democracy would indicate that the government was falling short of its aspirations and its intentions."[18] At the same time, however, both public order and the very survival of the regime were at stake. As Betancourt's minister of interior relations, Carlos Andrés Pérez, was to recall during his own successful campaign in 1973, the government was involved in a virtual war with anti-system revolutionaries committed to the use of violence and force. For the embattled Betancourt, the fundamental issue of elected democratic government required staunch and unyielding defense from his administration. In providing this, he remained within constitutional boundaries to the utmost degree possible, and when pushed to actions that may have transgressed such lines did so in the knowledge that he enjoyed public approval as well as the tacit acceptance of opposition political parties. In his handling of such a crucial and politically volatile problem, moreover, the president also demonstrated extraordinary leadership talents and skills.

## The Presidency of Raúl Leoni

If Betancourt's tough, pugnacious, even aggressive, personal style was appropriate for the tenor of the times, much the same might be suggested of his long-time colleague and associate Raúl Leoni. A sturdy adeco partisan throughout his career, Leoni was by personal inclination a quiet, taciturn, almost phlegmatic figure. Combined with a self-effacing shyness, this was to produce a president well suited to lead the nation in the wake of the terrorist years. The FALN campaign had collapsed following its failure to prevent elections and topple the constitutional regime. Leoni's broad task in a sense became one of presiding over a more tranquil period of normalization, one in which the diminution of AD strength and the rise of party opposition required quiet conciliation and increasingly nonpartisan leadership. This was typified by the debate over Venezuelan entry into the Latin American Free Trade Association (LAFTA).[19]

Betancourt had hoped to enter LAFTA before the close of his term, but sharp divisions within Fedecámaras made impossible the private sector consensus that he sought. He did create a mixed public-private study commission as a means of increasing support for LAFTA membership; in 1964 Leoni continued to pursue the matter. Yet Fedecámaras remained divided on the matter, choosing not to act at its June 1964 assembly. Leoni therefore began to prod the business sector, first announcing at the closing session that his government was planning to join LAFTA within a matter of months. Antagonistic forces promptly undertook their own campaign, including a spate of news releases alleging the defects of LAFTA. During the remainder of 1964 the debate continued, and the prointegration consensus sought by the president did not emerge. Faced with an opposition-controlled Congress, quiet and private persuasion became the order of the day.

Only at the close of the 1965 legislative session in November did Leoni finally submit enabling legislation authorizing him to ratify Venezuelan adherence to the Treaty of Montevideo, which had originally established the Latin American Free Trade Association. By that time the president had patched together the Ancha Base alliance with the URD and FND, greatly strengthening his position in Congress. Through bargaining and discussion with private sector leaders, he agreed to accept Venezuelan membership only if hedged by a number of conditions. This exchange of concessions and the interplay of countervailing pressures eventually led to congressional ratification on June 30, 1966, with Leoni promulgating the decree the following month. Thus, the eventual outcome, although broadly consistent with the president's objectives, had been realized only through vigorous consensus building with opposing forces that recognized the strength and vitality of the private sector. Without such bargaining Leoni's policy would have been rejected. The reality of political conditions at the time prohibited any exercise of raw presidential authority.

## The Presidency of Rafael Caldera

In 1969 Rafael Caldera brought to the presidency his own political ideology, policy preferences, and personal style of leadership. The creator and dominant leader of the Social Christian COPEI, Caldera in stature and appearance was every inch the president. Combining his political career with distinguished achievement as a writer and intellectual, he brought to the office an image of dignity, authority, and great competence. Having long held internal party matters in his own hands, moreover, Caldera similarly preferred a firmness in presidential decision making to compromise, unlike his predecessor. This was reflected in his decision not to rule through a multiparty coalition. Yet, Caldera was sensitive to his party's minority position, and often had little choice but to respond to the inevitable pressures. Three policy issues

during his administration help shed further light upon the dynamics of Venezuelan presidential power: adoption of "ideological pluralism" in foreign policy,[20] the 1969 debate over the executive's constitutional appointive powers,
and the political struggle eventually leading to the 1971 Hydrocarbons Reversion Law.

Of these, perhaps the first represented the most fundamental shift of
policy. The comparative freedom of action in the realm of international affairs
permitted Caldera a free hand. Since 1959 a hallmark of policy had been the
so-called Betancourt doctrine, whereby Venezuela withheld diplomatic recognition from illegitimate regimes. Designed as a symbolic tribute to constitutional government, its practical effect was the absence of diplomatic ties with
many Latin American regimes. President Caldera, whose writings had extended the Social Christian concept of social justice to the international sphere,
adopted ideological pluralism as the cornerstone of his foreign policy. His
March 1969 inaugural address announced his intention of changing "the
policy of discontinuing relations with regimes arising from acts of violence
against duly elected authorities on this continent."[21] Diplomatic ties were
renewed with a number of countries in the next few months, an action provoking little criticism.

Such unfettered executive authority was absent from domestic policy,
however. The conflict over presidential appointive powers, for one, had been
initiated by an AD-inspired bill transferring judicial appointive power beneath
the Supreme Court level from the minister of justice to a special committee.
Membership of the latter was so described as to give Acción Democrática
control. The measure was highly partisan, and Caldera strongly objected on
both constitutional and political grounds. When he vetoed the bill and returned it for reconsideration, the Delegated Commission—controlled by opposition forces—called Congress into special session; the bill was consequently
modified only slightly. Once again the president rejected the bill, and Congress
overrode his objections. Caldera then asked the Supreme Court to rule on the
constitutionality of the law, and his objections were rejected by a vote of 8 to
7. Two broad lessons were suggested: that constitutional constraints upon
Venezuelan presidents are not meaningless if the opposition has enough votes,
and that the dynamics of partisan politics cannot be ignored or denied even
by the firmest of executive actions.

The unfolding of discussions that led to the Hydrocarbons Reversion Law
was lengthy and complicated; it has been well described elsewhere.[22] Suffice
it to say that much of the initiative again came from Congress, where the
Movimiento Electoral del Pueblo first advanced the bill. Initially COPEI and
Acción Democrática entertained serious reservations about the proposal, both
as to content and constitutionality. Eventually the adeco legislative caucus
decided to support the bill, concluding that it would be difficult to oppose
politically. The president was concerned about the constitutional question and

displeased by a lack of consultation during the drafting of the legislation. His party's secretary-general proposed at one juncture the creation of a special commission of jurists to study and improve the bill. Eventually, however, Caldera decided to accept the measure and then swiftly became a vigorous and vocal champion of reversion. Congress duly passed, and the president signed, the bill. As a consequence, both political support and public opinion reached an enthusiastic nationalistic consensus, while the administration benefitted politically. In the process, of course, an important policy decision had been adopted and enacted. Approval of reversion had provided evidence of the flexibility and effectiveness of the system and of Caldera's capacity to operate within its boundaries.

## The Presidency of Carlos Andrés Pérez

President Pérez provides but the most recent example of leadership style. A man of great energy and unflagging drive, Carlos Andrés Pérez swiftly stamped his personal brand on the presidency. The use of decree powers has been evident under his incumbency, and critics have charged him with abusing executive authority, although rarely citing specific cases. Nevertheless, Pérez has not pushed to the limits his potential power. For one thing, his stature as party leader of Acción Democrática is less overwhelming than that of Caldera had been with COPEI. There have been tensions between the AD leadership and the president almost from the outset. This has sometimes been ascribed to an inadequacy of his consultation with party leaders; be that as it may, Pérez does not always find the party uniformly responsive to or dependent upon his decisions.

As with his predecessors, Pérez has found ample room for maneuver in foreign policy. An exemplary instance was his decision to restore relations with Havana and champion Cuba's reincorporation into the hemispheric family of nations. Although subjected to periodic criticism—especially following the intervention of Cuban troops in Angola—the policy remained in effect.

With domestic issues, in contrast, Pérez has demonstrated a strong preference for securing multiparty support of major decisions. Whether a product of the declining tradition of an omnipotent presidency or more simply a function of political calculation, Pérez has sometimes exerted himself mightily on behalf of broad consensus. The nationalization of oil is a case in point. During his 1973 campaign Pérez had promised not to *"petrolizar las elecc-iones,"* and his inaugural address of March 12, 1974 pledged his government to fix oil policy on a national rather than partisan basis. A 36-man presidential commission of petroleum reversion was swiftly created, composed of representatives of several political parties, business interests, and trade unions. Late in 1974 the commission presented a detailed draft to the president, and in March

1975 the government introduced legislation to Congress for debate and discussion. The controversial Article 5, whereby the government was to be authorized to sign agreements of association with private enterprise under certain conditions, proved the rock on which consensus foundered. Ultimately, the administration was forced to gain approval of the legislation by application of party discipline in the congressional vote. Only one minor party also voted for the bill. The issues related to Article 5 are of great importance to Venezuela, but depart from our present theme. What is relevant here was the president's decision to seek a national consensus on the matter. First rejecting the easy path of enacting the measure by executive decree, as was permissible through the Hydrocarbons Reversion Law of 1971, he also undertook to win legislative approval of the opposition. Although ultimately unsuccessful, the administration pursued consensus for several months. For Pérez, in this case, the strongest form of presidential authority had not been used, and even the reliance upon party control of Congress was employed only after all avenues of approach to the opposition had led to an impasse.

## The Role of Personal Style

Such illustrations could be multiplied at length to support the contention that personal leadership style is uniformly relevant. Certainly the personal and political status of any president is important, and expecially his standing as a national party leader. Of the last four presidents, Raúl Leoni was relatively the least strong in this context. While an eminent adeco leader with substantial personal credentials, he reached the presidency at a time when the party had been weakened by two divisions and a third was brewing. Furthermore, his predecessor had enjoyed higher status as a party and national leader. In contrast to Leoni, both Betancourt and Caldera reached the presidency as acknowledged caudillos of their respective parties.

Betancourt, major founder and organizer of the AD, provisional president from 1945–48, and symbolic leader of the hemisphere's "democratic left," had operated from a strong party base. His standing with COPEI and with lesser opposition parties augmented his ability to exercise national direction. Caldera was even more dominant within his own party. For two decades he had almost single-handedly built COPEI from a small, narrowly-based sectarian group into a major national force, one which by 1968 had become the most responsive and best organized in Venezuela. Caldera's position was therefore of inestimable value to his administration, especially faced with an opposition majority in Congress.

Pérez assumed office with the momentum of the greatest electoral victory in contemporary times. While such senior AD figures as Gonzalo Barrios and

Betancourt himself remained active, the mantle of party leadership had been passed to a new generation. Carlos Andrés Pérez, after a career of party service and five years as secretary-general, moved to Miraflores Palace as a highly popular figure. There he enjoyed the advantages of unified party support—at least at the outset—and a clear popular mandate. Both his political opportunities and national responsibilities were great, and the bases for strong presidential leadership were more substantial than those of any of his three predecessors.

## CONCLUSIONS

Since 1958 the tradition of unbridled presidential authority has diminished noticeably.[23] This is not to deny that the existing system is clearly presidential; certainly the role of chief of state remains constitutionally dominant, and each of the system's four presidents have, in their individual fashions, provided strong and firm guidance in the formulation and implementation of policy. At the same time, significant constraints are produced by national political conditions. There has been a consistent recognition and acceptance of the need for those limitations implied by the commitment to democratic processes. The result has been the implantation of a new tradition—still in its formative period—that views the president as subject to the limitations of other political forces.

Such brakes on the executive may be expected to become more broadly institutionalized in future years. In constitutional terms, this has largely revolved about proposed amendments to existing provisions concerning more than one term per person. One recent suggestion has called for a single six-year term and ineligibility for a second. This has sometimes been tied to proposals for congressional changes as well, including the introduction of staggered elections and two-year terms for members of the lower chamber. A variation that has been discussed for some time proposes retention of the five-year term, but without the possibility of a second one ten years later. Proposals to prohibit multiple terms were debated extensively in 1972 and 1973, but largely as a means of preventing a possible return to office by Marcos Pérez Jiménez. A related proposal has called for a runoff between the two leading presidential vote-getters should no candidate win 50 percent. This reform was raised after both the Leoni and Caldera elections when the winners received but 33 and 20 percent respectively. The magnitude of the Pérez victory at least temporarily laid to rest the proposal.

Whether or not these or related constitutional amendments are adopted, the practical facts of political life can be expected to remain. The impact of party rule is one such reality. If, as some argue, the 1973 election results augur the emergence of a two-party system, a president can be assured of strong, articulate, and well-organized opposition. And should the earlier predilection for multiple parties return, it will be difficult for any executive to enjoy an outright majority, in which case coalitions and alliances will be necessary. In either event, bargaining and compromise will be inevitable. As to presidential stature and status, it may well be that the era of such powerfully dominant leaders as Betancourt and Caldera is passing. Contemporary politicians will be unable to build unchallenged leadership through experiences such as those the party founders lived through. Similarly, total authority within a major political party will be more difficult to attain.

The increasing political skill of major interest groups can also be expected to enforce the limitations placed upon the chief of state. Combined with the growing political sophistication of a citizenry already knowledgeable about such matters, the impact of personalism may well decline. To varying degrees, each of the four presidents has been a civilian caudillo, yet none could rule unchallenged. Even domination over his own party has sometimes eluded a president. Thus, Rómulo Betancourt was not heeded in his stated preference for a nominee other than Raúl Leoni in 1963. And while Rafael Caldera was successful in obtaining the candidacy of Lorenzo Fernández as a potential successor, he later failed to prevent the emergence of Luis Herrera Campins as probable copeyano candidate for 1978. Carlos Andrés Pérez has encountered strong opposition from his party's national executive committee on several occasions, such as the official AD rejection of the five-year Plan of the Nation first announced by his economic advisers in early 1976.

Venezuelan presidential power, in sum, has experienced an institutionalization and acceptance of both constitutional and informal limitations since 1958. The present democratic system, having persisted for nearly two decades, has produced precisely those constraints customarily associated with political pluralism. A fundamental change of regime—as, for example, a nonelected military government—would reverse the prevailing trend. So long as the existing system endures, however, its characteristics are likely to become increasingly embedded in national attitudes and values. No president will be immune to the formal and informal limitations implied by democratic pluralism.

## NOTES

1. Ramón Escovar Salom, *Evolución política de Venezuela* (Caracas: Monte Avila, Editores, 1972), p. 94.

2. These words of Antonio Guzmán Blanco, recorded by Antonio Arraiz, are cited by Juan Liscano in "Aspectos de la vida social y política de Venezuela," *150 Años de vida republicana (1811-1961)* (Caracas: Ediciones de la Presidencia de la República, 1963), p. 191.

3. This point is developed more fully by José Agustín Silva Michelena in his *The Illusion of Democracy in Dependent Nations* (Cambridge, Mass.:MIT Press, 1971), pp. 45-49.

4. The standard English treatments are Thomas Rourke, *Gómez: Tyrant of the Andes* (New York: Morrow, 1941); and John Lavin, *A Halo for Gómez* (New York: Pageant Press, 1954). The

Venezuelan literature is extensive, and much of it of a high quality. There has been a recent revival of interest in Gómez, as suggested by lengthy essays in *Resumen* (Caracas) during 1975.

5. Guillermo Morón, *A History of Venezuela,* ed. and trans. John Street (New York: Roy, 1963), pp. 192–93.

6. Laureano Vallenilla Lanz, *Cesarismo democrático,* 3d ed. (Caracas: Garrido, 1952). The original edition appeared in 1929.

7. For detailed treatment see María de Lourdes Acedo de Sucre and Carmen Margarita Nones Mendoza, *La generación venezolana de 1928: estudio de una élite política* (Caracas: Ediciones Ariel, 1967). A briefer summary is John D. Martz, "Venezuela's 'Generation of 28' : The Genesis of Political Democracy," *Journal of Inter-American Studies* 6 (1964): 17–33.

8. Extensive discussion of these activities is found in John D. Martz, *Acción Democrática: Evolution of a Modern Political Party in Venezuela* (Princeton: Princeton University Press, 1966).

9. For a broad, multi-authored assessment of the post-1958 period, see John D. Martz and David J. Myers, eds., *Venezuela: The Democratic Experience* (forthcoming).

10. Daniel H. Levine, *Conflict and Political Change in Venezuela* (Princeton: Princeton University Press, 1973).

11. This is examined more fully in Frank Tugwell, *The Politics of Oil in Venezuela* (Palo Alto, Calif.: Stanford University Press, 1975), esp. pp. 118–20.

12. See John D. Martz, "Values, Consensus, and Policy-Making: Oil Nationalization in Venezuela," forthcoming.

13. John D. Martz, "The Growth and Democratization of the Venezuelan Labor Movement," *Inter-American Economic Affairs* 17 (1963): 3–18.

14. The fullest account is John Duncan Powell, *Political Mobilization of the Venezuelan Peasant* (Cambridge, Mass.: Harvard University Press, 1971).

15. Charles W. Anderson, "Reformmongering and the Uses of Political Power," *Inter-American Economic Affairs* 19 (1965): 25–42.

16. Relevant portions of the data appear in John D. Martz and Enrique A. Baloyra, *Political Mobilization and Participation: The Venezuelan Campaign of 1973* (Chapel Hill: University of North Carolina Press, 1976), esp. intro. and chap. 9.

17. A close account appears in Robert J. Alexander, *The Venezuelan Democratic Revolution: A Profile of the Regime of Rómulo Betancourt* (New Brunswick: Rutgers University Press, 1964), pp. 118–36.

18. Ibid., p. 307.

19. This case is outlined by Robert P. Clark, Jr., "Economic Integration and the Political Process: Linkage Politics in Venezuela," in Philip B. Taylor, Jr., ed., *Venezuela: 1969: Analysis of Progress* (Washington, D.C.: The Johns Hopkins University, 1971), pp. 216–37.

20. Among his many discussions of the subject, see Rafael Caldera, *El bloque latinoamericano,* 2d ed (Mérida: Universidad de los Andes, 1966); *Especificidad de la democracia cristiana* (Barcelona: Editorial Nova Terra, 1973); and *Justicia social internacional y nacionalismo latinoamericano* (Madrid: Seminarios y Ediciones, 1973).

21. Rafael Caldera, *Discurso a la nación* (Caracas: Imprenta Nacional, 1969).

22. See Tugwell, op. cit.

23. An excellent discussion of the earlier tradition of presidential authority is Leo B. Lott, "Executive Power in Venezuela," *The American Political Science Review* 50 (1956): 422–41. A more contemporary view is George W. Grayson, "Venezuela's Presidential Politics," *Current History* 66 (1974).

# INDEX

# ABOUT THE EDITOR AND
# THE CONTRIBUTORS

THOMAS V. DIBACCO is Associate Professor of History and Dean for Faculty Affairs at the American University, Washington, D.C. He began his teaching career at the University of South Florida, Tampa, in 1964. Dr. DiBacco has published widely in the area of U.S. history, and his articles and reviews have appeared in the *American Historical Review, Business History Review, Journal of American History,* and the *Review of Politics.*

ROBERT J. ALEXANDER is Professor of Economics at Rutgers University, New Brunswick, New Jersey, where he has taught since 1947. He has also served as a visiting professor at several universities and as an advisor and consultant to various public and private agencies. Dr. Alexander has published many books on Latin American economics and politics; his most recent, *A New Development Strategy,* was published in 1976.

ROBERT H. DIX is Professor of Political Science at Rice University, Houston, Texas. He has taught at Yale University and served as a political officer of the U.S. Embassy at Bogotá, Colombia. Dr. Dix's major publications include *Colombia: The Political Dimensions of Change* (1967) and *Colombia's Response to Violence: Essays on a Coalition Regime* (co-author, 1976).

KENNETH F. JOHNSON is Associate Professor of Political Science at the University of Missouri-St. Louis. Until 1970 he was Associate Professor of Political Science and Chairman, Latin American Studies Program, at the University of Southern California, Los Angeles. Dr. Johnson has published numerous articles in scholarly journals, and his books include *Mexican Democracy: A Critical View* (1972) and *Guerrilla Politics on the Argentine Left* (1975).

HARRY KANTOR is Professor Emeritus of Political Science at Marquette University, Milwaukee, Wisconsin, where he taught from 1968 until his retirement in 1976. He also taught for 16 years at the University of Florida and served for many years as associate and managing editor of the *Journal of Politics.* The author of more than 50 journal articles, Dr. Kantor has published several books on Latin American politics, including *The Costa Rican Election of 1953: A Case Study* (1958) and *Patterns of Politics and Political Systems in Latin America* (1969).

JOHN D. MARTZ is Professor of Political Science at the University of North Carolina, Chapel Hill, and editor of the *Latin American Research*

*Review.* He also served as chairman of UNC's Department of Political Science from 1970–75. Dr. Martz's extensive publications range from a book on Ecuador and two recent volumes on Venezuela to works on *Latin American Political Thought and Ideology* (co-author, 1970) and *Dynamics of Change in Latin American Politics* (1971).

KENNETH J. MIJESKI is Associate Professor of Political Science at East Tennessee State University, Johnson City, where he has taught since 1971. His teaching fields include comparative politics with emphasis on Latin America, political psychology, and the politics of the developing nations. Dr. Mijeski is the co-author of a Sage Research paper on Chile and Costa Rica and co-organizer of a summer study program in Mexico.

VENEZUELA: THE DEMOCRATIC EXPERIENCE
edited by
John D. Martz
David J. Myers

ALLENDE'S CHILE
edited by
Philip O'Brien

THE INTER-AMERICAN DEVELOPMENT BANK
AND POLITICAL INFLUENCE: With Special
Reference to Costa Rica
R. Peter DeWitt, Jr.

THE UNITED STATES AND MILITARISM IN
CENTRAL AMERICA
Don L. Etchison